Pedigree

Published by Pedigree in association with Yours
Pedigree Books Limited, Beech House, Walnut Gardens, Exeter, Devon EX4 4DH

Yours – the read of your life every fortnight! Look out for it in your local newsagent.
Yours – Bauer London Lifestyle, Media House, Peterborough Business Park, Peterborough PE2 6EA.
Tel: 01733 468000

Compiled and edited by Caroline Chadderton
Designed by David Reid
Sub-edited by Christine Curtis
Additional writing by Marion Clarke, Sharon Reid, Rebecca Speechley, Sheena Correa
and gardening expert Gareth Salter

With grateful thanks to the following:
Garden Answers, The Blackcurrant Foundation, The Watercress Alliance, www.allaboutoats.com, Splenda®,
www.meatmatters.com, Gold Top milk, Nestlé Carnation, Tenderstem® broccoli,
www.wholegraingoodness.com, British Asparagus Growers' Association,
Belvoir Fruit Farms, Anchor butter, www.thefreerangebutter.co.uk, The British Potato Council,
UK Salad Producers, www.nzlambrecipes.info, www.mushroom-uk.com, www.lovepork.co.uk,
www.discoverkale.co.uk, www.anchorsquirtymoments.co.uk, The Goose Fat Information Service

**Special thanks once again to the readers who have contributed so wonderfully to this Year Book
by sending in their memories, precious photographs, stories and tips**

◆ If you're unsure about taking up any of the advice in the Healthier for Longer section,
especially if you are on medication – please check it out with your GP

◆ All telephone numbers, website details and dates correct at time of going to press

Welcome to the 2009 Yours Yearbook . It truly is Yours, because without the memories and photographs that poured in from Yours readers it would be a very slim volume!

You've shared your magical stories of grandparents and schooldays – and entrusted us with wonderful black and white photographs that conjure up a lost world. And an amazing number of you have had close encounters of the celebrity kind and have interesting stories to tell. And if your memory or story didn't make it in – thanks so much anyway, we thoroughly enjoyed reading every one and it wasn't an easy decision to make.

But we've also managed to pack in recipes and tips, health snippets and information on your favourite garden plants and shrubs. And there are a few surprises as well, that I won't give away, to keep your interest throughout the year.

Happy reading – and all the best for a peaceful 2009

Valery

Valery McConnell
Editor, **Yours**

PS A big thank you to Caroline Chadderton and her team of helpers without whom, the Yours Yearbook would not exist.

£6.99

January 2009

Thursday
1
New Year's Day

Friday
2

Saturday
3

Sunday
4

Monday
5

Tuesday
6
Epiphany

Wednesday
7

Thursday
8

Friday
9

Saturday
10

Sunday
11

Monday
12

Tuesday
13

Wednesday
14

Thursday
15

Friday
16

Saturday
17

Sunday
18

Monday
19

Tuesday
20

Wednesday
21

Thursday
22

Friday 23	**Wednesday** 28
Saturday 24	**Thursday** 29
Sunday 25 Burns' Night	**Friday** 30
Monday 26 Chinese New Year (Year of the Ox)	**Saturday** 31
Tuesday 27 Holocaust Memorial Day	

Behind the Scenes

After the Fox, 1966

Even stars have to eat… Here we see Peter Sellers and Britt Ekland having lunch between takes on the set of the 1966 film comedy, After the Fox. While Britt's food is untouched, she seems to find something good to eat on Peter's plate.

Goon Show and Pink Panther star Peter was married to Britt from 1964 to 1968; they appear in the film as brother and sister. But despite the film's pedigree line-up – distinguished Italian director Vittoria De Sica, a screenplay by

American writer Neil Simon, Peter as master criminal (and master of disguise) Aldo Vanucci (aka The Fox) and a great performance by Victor Mature as an ageing Hollywood hunk – it didn't set the film world alight.

But since then, the story of the hijacking of $3 million in gold bullion in Cairo, and trying to smuggle it into Europe, has taken on a cult following, poking fun as it does at film directors, movie stars and critics.

My Grandparents

My paternal grandfather was Edward Hill and he married Emma Oliver on April 26, 1891. They lived in Shamley Green, Surrey and in 1951, celebrated their Diamond wedding anniversary, which was covered by The Surrey Advertiser and the London Evening Standard.

Edward and Emma – and a goose!

I was 10 when my parents parted and my mother and I went to live with my maternal grandparents.

I have so many happy memories of running round the well in the garden but, at that age, I was very wary of the geese. Unfortunately, after my parents parted, I did not see my Granny and Granddad for almost ten years but when we eventually met up again, nothing had changed, they were still the loving couple I'd remembered through those missing years. **Maureen Brown, Sheerness, Kent**

Colourful climbers

Garrya elliptica

Called the silk tassel bush because of its male catkins, the most popular variety is 'James Roof', which is laden with elegant long tassels during winter and early spring. Although nominally hardy, it benefits from a sheltered position, so plant it against a warm wall. It thrives in full sun or partial shade, may reach 3m in height and copes in most soils. Plants widely available.

Cookery for you

BLACKCURRANT SMOOTHIE

Serves 1

- ◆ 110 g (4 oz) fresh or frozen blackcurrants
- ◆ 1 small ripe banana
- ◆ 200 ml (7 fl oz) apple juice
- ◆ 2 tablespoons plain yoghurt

1. Chop up the banana into small chunks.
2. Tip all the ingredients into a food processor or blender and blend until smooth.
3. Pour into a glass and serve.

Recipe courtesy The Blackcurrant Foundation

▮ THAT'S INTERESTING…

England didn't adopt January 1 as New Year's Day until 1752, more than 150 years after Scotland. Before that the year began on March 25, (which was the feast of the Annunciation).

Schooldays remembered

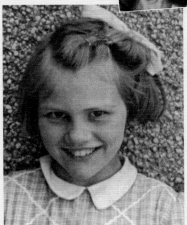

I was seven in 1947 when my parents moved from Yorkshire to Llandudno, and I didn't want to go because it meant leaving my friends behind.

There were no school buses, so our milkman took the neighbourhood children on his horse and cart after he'd finished his round. He'd take us to the school's back entrance, down an alleyway.

On the first day, I jumped down from the cart and took in the strange surroundings - on the left were stables, with two horses in the stalls. The milkman had gone and I was alone…

I didn't know the children and I didn't want to go to this new school, so I ducked into the stables. It was warm in the hay; I wasn't sleeping well, so I slept some of the time. When I heard the playtime bell, I'd go out and find the toilet, then pop back into the stables.

After a while, my mother had a visit from the School Board, wanting to know why she hadn't taken me to school. She promptly told the two men that I went on the

Sandra in June 1950

milk cart every morning and she collected me in the afternoon.

Before long they were back to report that I wasn't registered at school; my mother said there must be some mistake and that my father would personally take me to school the next day.

I was put on the cart as usual but, unknown to me, my father followed behind on his bicycle. Of course, my secret was soon discovered - Sandra Holmes shall go to school!

**Sandra Jones,
Llandudno, Gwynedd**

Healthier for longer!

Get healthy now – it's never too late to increase your odds of living longer according to US scientists. Quitting smoking, eating a healthy diet and taking regular exercise could increase your life expectancy even if you don't start until your 50s, 60s, 70s or 80s.

Meeting the stars

In 2006, my grandson Matthew, then aged two, loved watching Buster the dog on Paul O'Grady's show, so my daughter wrote asking that his name be put in the draw to hopefully receive a nodding Buster. To her surprise, the studio phoned her asking about Matthew, and she mentioned that he had a toy dog on wheels that resembled Buster.

The three of us (plus dog on wheels!) were invited to the studios and we had the pleasure of meeting Paul, Buster and Olga. Although we were nervous, he quickly put us at our ease, being so friendly and charming. And Matthew got his nodding Buster!

Maureen Sims, Ashford, Kent

Left: Paul with Maureen and Matthew

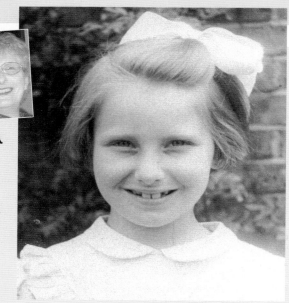

Schooldays remembered

The school I went to from 1952 until 1959 was All Saints Infants and Juniors School, Church Street, Edmonton.

Sadly, this old redbrick building no longer stands. Gone are the open fires attended to by the school caretaker, where frozen milk would thaw in the winter and in summer would turn to cheese by the empty grate. Gone is the hall where the Christmas parties were held; bring your own plate, cup and saucer with your name on – my mum used sticky plasters.

Outside, a walnut tree stood in the corner of the playground, not very interesting to us girls but irresistible to the boys. It was out of bounds and anyone found up it was straightaway sent to see the headmistress.

To reach the school, I had to walk down a lane, and in the beginning my mum would take me on the

Rosalind has fond memories of her old school

ten minute walk, but from the age of seven I did it on my own. On my left was the old overgrown orchard and on my right the graveyard to All Saints Church. Pleasant enough in the summer but on misty autumn days and dark winter mornings, it was not a place you wanted to dawdle.

Rosalind Wicker, London N21

My Grandparents

My Granddad was a Chief Superintendent of police in County Durham, living in a large house connected by doorways to the station, together with law courts and cells – and in 1940 we were evacuated there from Coventry.

I was nine, and what joy awaited me and my six-year-old sister, Joyce. No thoughts of air-raids or war, but lost puppies and dogs in the 'pound', large tennis courts and our school right next door to the 'cop shop'!

The days were wonderful, as the policemen took us to their

hearts and we had sweets and toys in abundance. We were there for more than two years and witnessed the heaviest snowfall ever. It was up to 5ft, over the outhouse door and we were stranded for four days until we were dug out.

Gran said that if we got our dollies out, we'd have our picture taken for the Consett News, but at the last minute Gran decided to hide behind the snow!

I'll never forget the wonderful days in Consett my Grandparents gave my sister and I.

Moira Round, Birmingham

Winter 1942: Moira and Joyce, with Gran somewhere behind the snow!

Cookery for you

WATERCRESS AND PEA RISOTTO

Serves 4

- ◆ 1 tablespoon olive oil
- ◆ 1 onion, finely chopped
- ◆ 1 clove garlic
- ◆ 400 g (13 oz) risotto rice
- ◆ 150 ml (¼ pint) dry white wine
- ◆ 750 ml (1¼ pints) hot vegetable stock
- ◆ 150 g (5 oz) frozen peas
- ◆ ½ teaspoon freshly grated nutmeg
- ◆ 1 x 110 g (4 oz) pack watercress, roughly chopped
- ◆ 25g (1 oz) freshly grated Parmesan cheese

1 Heat the oil in a large heavy pan, add the onion and sauté for 4 minutes, until soft but not coloured. Add the garlic and rice and cook for 1 more minute, stirring.
2 Add the white wine and stir for 2-3 mins until most of the liquid has been absorbed. Add a ladle of the stock and cook for 2-3 mins, stirring occasionally to prevent sticking until the liquid has been absorbed. Repeat until you have just a little stock left and the rice is almost tender.
3 Add the remaining stock, peas, nutmeg and cook until the rice is soft and creamy. Remove from the heat. Add the watercress and cheese and season to taste. Serve immediately.

Recipe courtesy The Watercress Alliance

Colourful climbers
Clematis armandii

Clematis armandii is one of the most desirable climbing plants because it produces delicious, almond-scented, white-pink flowers in early spring that shine out against green bronze-tinted leaves. Vigorous and evergreen, it enjoys a sunny, west- or south-facing site. Plant it by a pathway and let its scent tantalise you on sunny winter days. It reaches 3m in height. Plants widely available.

TOP TIP

If you're making a sausage sandwich, cut the sausages up for easier eating (and it's quicker with scissors).

Healthier for longer!

Eat more whole grains – such oats and whole grain bread and cereals. They could help you avoid chronic diseases such as diabetes and heart disease, by lowering your body weight and reducing inflammation.

THAT'S INTERESTING...

An 'IOU' is a note and acknowledgement of person debt, the acronym stands for 'Is Owed Unto'.

Cookery for you

FRESH FRUIT COMPOTE

Serves 4

- ◆ 1 dessert apple, cored and sliced
- ◆ 1 pear, cored and sliced
- ◆ 4 plums, halved and stoned
- ◆ 1 vanilla pod
- ◆ 150 ml (¼ pint) red wine mixed with 150 ml (¼ pint) water
- ◆ 3 tablespoons Splenda® granulated sweetener

1 Preheat the oven to 180°C/fan oven 160°C/Gas Mark 4. Place all the ingredients in an ovenproof dish with a lid and cook for 45 minute, or until the fruit is tender.

2 Leave to cool slightly before serving warm or chilling until required.

Tip: Serve with a scoop of vanilla ice cream, or with a dollop of Greek yoghurt.

Recipe courtesy Splenda®, www.splenda.co.uk

Colourful climbers
Hedera 'Kolibri'

A trusted evergreen climber that's great at encouraging wildlife in the garden, this ivy cultivar has large, creamy variegated leaves. It's great in shade and will cling to fences, walls and trellis with ease, so there's no need to provide support. Quick-growing, it copes in most soils and situations, and can reach several metres in height. Prune it regularly to keep it within bounds. Plants widely available.

My Grandparents

From left: Joyce's Gran, her Mum, two aunts and her Granddad

My Gran and Granddad lived in Mill Cottage, Longstock, Hampshire, a pretty thatched cottage beside the River Test. They collected all their water in white enamel buckets and could drink it without boiling it because it was so pure, and Granddad would catch eels in the river.

There was just one room downstairs in the cottage and two bedrooms at the top of twisty stairs.

Gran made lots of jam and always gave my sister and I tiny sample pots of it to take home.

Joyce Gowman, Amesbury, Wilts

Schooldays remembered

Margaret, aged 8 in 1948

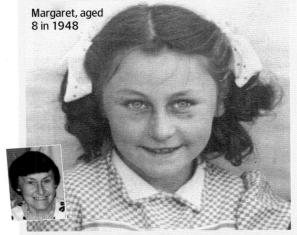

I learned how to spell CHRYSANTHEMUM when I was eight, and I wished I hadn't. My parents were born in the 1890s and spelling was important in their schools, so I had spelling tests on birds, rivers and flowers. My father's prize bloom, both gardening and spelling-wise, was chrysanthemum.

I enjoyed the spelling tests at junior school in Beverley, East Yorkshire, especially the day when the pièce de résistance was CHRYSANTHEMUM. Miss Johnson was surprised when I spelt it correctly. Unfortunately, the top girls had stumbled on MARIGOLD, so they held out no hope for CHRYSANTHEMUM.

To my embarrassment, at the age of eight, I was paraded in front of them, to humiliate them with my correct spelling. What was worse was then being put up a class. 'Clever Dick,' they called me to begin with but by whispering correct answers to my classmates, I curried favour and became reasonably happy.

Handicraft lessons were on two afternoons a week and knitting played a prominent part.

At school, my pink wool vest grew apace, and I duly did the cast-off for the square neck. Progress down the back was boringly slow, so I pulled the side seam very taut to match the front side seam, then was given the go-ahead to sew it up.

Having paid two shillings for it, I was expected to wear it. It itched, shrank in the wash and never warmed my back owing to my economy.

Margaret Walker, Porthmadog, Gwynedd

Healthier for longer!

Get a cat - owning a moggy could reduce your risk of having a heart attack by a third by soothing anxiety and lowering your stress levels, according to scientists at the University of Minnesota.

THAT'S INTERESTING...

If you heat a lemon (30 seconds in a microwave) you'll get more juice out of it.

Meeting the stars

In August 1983 I went to see Barry Manilow in concert at Blenheim Palace. In the second half, he asked for someone to go on stage to sing with him, and I was the lucky lady he chose. I sang Can't Smile Without You and was rewarded with a hug, two kisses and a signed T-shirt saying I Sang With Barry Manilow.

I had some publicity in several newspapers, a local radio interview and a TV interview on Central TV News. To cap it all, he'd written about it in his autobiography!

Cath Greenwell, Hinckley, Leics

Cath and Barry in concert!

TOP TIP

Keep a list of library books you've enjoyed, so you can look for other books by the same author – and recommend them to friends.

Schooldays remembered

I went to Beckenham Grammar School for Girls, aged 11 in 1949 and will be forever grateful for the stability and firm platform for future life that our school provided. The school timetable catered for all abilities, with teaching of a high standard.

The many activities included orchestras and choirs, drama, school council, field club, debating society, drama, gymnastic competitions, Christmas carol concert and an annual Gilbert and Sullivan production.

These were some of the happiest years of my life and our active old girls' association hosts an annual lunch for a gathering of fond reminiscences and nostalgia.

I read a quote once, 'There is something infinitely comforting about being with someone who remembers you in your Aertex shirt and navy gym knickers'.

Janet Lambert, Longfield, Kent

Above: Janet in 1957, Below: Janet (extreme left) and her schoolfriends celebrating their first outing 50 years ago

Cookery for you

HEATHER HONEY PORRIDGE

Serves 4

- ◆ 120 g (4½ oz) pinhead oatmeal
- ◆ 500 ml (approx 1 pint) water
- ◆ 500 ml (approx 1 pint) semi-skimmed milk (and a little extra if needed)
- ◆ 2 tablespoons heather honey
- ◆ 2 tablespoons low fat crème fraîche
- ◆ A drizzle of honey, to serve (optional)

1 If you have the time, soak the oatmeal in the water for 10-15 minutes beforehand in a saucepan. Then add the milk and put the pan on a medium heat.

2 Bring to the boil, then reduce the heat and simmer for 6-10 minutes, stirring occasionally. Stir in the heather honey. Add a touch more milk or water, to achieve the consistency you prefer.

3 Pour the mixture into 4 bowls. Top each bowlful with ½ tablespoon of crème fraîche, and a drizzle of honey. Serve immediately.

Recipe courtesy www.allaboutoats.com

▌ THAT'S INTERESTING...

Rain is liquid precipitation in the form of water drops. Drops with a diameter of less than half a millimetre are known as drizzle.

Healthier for longer!

Work out your Body Mass Index (BMI) – it will tell you if you're a healthy weight for your height. Divide your weight in kilogrammes by your height in metres squared. If you're 1.6m (5ft 3in) tall and weigh 65kg (10st 3lb). The calculation would be 1.6 x 1.6 = 2.56. Then 65 divided by 2.56 = 25.39. A BMI of 18.5 and 24.9 is healthy – anything above that could increase your risk of heart disease, diabetes and even some cancers.

TOP TIP

To remove bobbles from jumpers, use an old razor and lightly shave.

My Grandparents

My grandparents, Florence and George Homan lived in a terraced house in Liverpool, not far from the football ground. The floors at the front of the house weren't level, and their bed was propped up with thick books at one end.

He worked for the GPO as a telephone engineer and drove a little green van with ladders on top. He was once working underground when a gas pipe burst and he was blown out onto the pavement. He was in hospital with burns but never had any scars – he was called 'The Miracle Man of Birkenhead' in the local paper.

There was a big bush in the garden which Granddad said was a banana tree. It was actually a hydrangea. Of course, we'd never seen bananas during the war and one year when Uncle Bert came home from sea, he brought a pile of tiny bananas in his kit bag.

Granddad sent us all away to play, then tied the bananas onto the bush. When we returned, we were allowed to pick them. I'll never forget my first banana, and we really believed that they had suddenly grown while we were out!

Grandma looked after the chickens, which were fed with a horrible smelling concoction which she cooked on the stove. Every Monday, Grandma and Aunty Betty did the washing, (with boiler, dolly tub and mangle) and on Tuesday she ironed, but Granddad's 'undies' were folded up and put between sheets of paper under the cushion on his chair – it was a weekly ritual. She always laughed and said, 'Let the old beggar do his own ironing!'.

**Audrey Rimmer,
Liverpool**

Grandma Florence
and Granddad George

Colourful climbers
Clematis cirrhosa 'Balearica'

The finely-cut foliage of this evergreen clematis is a delight all year round but even more so when tinted bronze during winter. A joy in early spring when covered in masses of fragrant flowers - usually between January and March - it benefits from being planted against a sheltered south or west-facing wall. Reaching only 3m in height, it makes a lovely container plant. Plants widely available.

Cookery for you

CINNAMON AND SPICED WINTER BERRIES ICE-CREAM

Serves 4

- ◆ 570 ml (1 pint approx) double cream
- ◆ 150 ml (¼ pint) Belvoir Spiced Winter Berries Cordial
- ◆ 110 g (4oz) cinnamon spiced biscuits

1 Whip the cream to a floppy 'custard-like' consistency.
2 Stir in the Belvoir Spiced Winter Berries cordial. The mixture will thicken considerably.
3 Crush the biscuits with your hands over the mixture.
4 Stir lightly, then spoon the mixture into individual bowls, or one large bowl, and freeze overnight.
5 Once out of the freezer, serve immediately.

Tip: Try putting the mixture in individual jelly moulds, as they freeze well and are easy to turn out.

Recipe courtesy Belvoir Fruit Farms

My Grandparents

Lisa's Grandma (standing back row, left) in her dancing troupe

'Grandma from by the Sea' - so called because we also had a Grandma in the country - oozed good nana kindness. My sister and I loved going to see her because she lived near the beach. But it was not just the sea and the kindness – she had a magic.

Grandma found it hard to concentrate on cooking and household chores, her food often burnt because she would read a book while preparing it. She loved films, too, and one of her favourites was The Red Shoes. She liked Gene Kelly, as Grandma had been a dancer in her youth, something I didn't get to know about until after she died.

After her death, Granddad occupied himself with winemaking and beekeeping, he also started to hoard and every space in the house in Whitstable became occupied. When Granddad died, the house was cleared, and it was then that a letter was found which Grandma had written a few years before she died,

'Oh, I wish I was 16 again. When I was 16, I was with a dancing troupe of girls, travelling the country, going by train from town to town each week.

The rooms behind the stage were cold and bare, and each Saturday our costumes were packed in big baskets called skips.

We only had one-and-a-half slices of bread a day for tea, and big mugs of cocoa made with thick sweetened condensed milk for supper.'

Grandma's advice was to make good use of your hidden talents. As a teenager, I wanted to be like Grandma by the Sea and I tried dancing, but I don't think that is my hidden gift.

Lisa Allen, Surbiton, Surrey

THAT'S INTERESTING...

The first patent for the bent wire paper clip was awarded to an American, Samuel B Fay in 1867.

TOP TIP

Rolling an orange around firmly on a firm surface should make it easier to peel.

Schooldays remembered

Joan in 1939, aged seven

I went to school during the war, and we had to use another school while air raid shelters were being built at ours. We shared schools, one week we went in the mornings, the next in the afternoons and thought it was great!

One winter during playtime I slipped on an icy patch and couldn't stand up. The headmaster came out and carried me into school; he thought I might have broken my leg, so he drove me home and asked the doctor to call.

The doctor confirmed that I'd broken it in two places. He opened his black bag, asked my mother for a bowl of warm water and proceeded to plaster my leg from foot to knee. I had instructions not to walk, and no school for six weeks – I was really upset as I loved school, and playing with my friends.

Joan McNamara, Coulsdon, Surrey

Healthier for longer!

Beat gout… by cutting down on soft drinks such as cola. Scientists have found that people who drink two or more servings of fizzy drinks a day increase their risk of gout by a shocking 85 per cent, compared to people who only indulge just once a month.

Colourful climbers
Clematis cirrhosa 'Freckles'

Similar in many ways to 'Balearica', the variety 'Freckles' is also worth growing because its creamy bell-shaped flowers are heavily freckled with red, ensuring it livens up even the gloomiest winter garden. And, with little else happening so early in spring, it looks wonderful when viewed through a window. Give it a sheltered position and it will flower happily between January and March, reaching 9m in height. Plants widely available.

Meeting the stars

I won first prize in a poetry competition run by Help the Aged and I am enjoying a celebratory lunch with Diane Moran, the fitness guru.

I not only won the posh lunch in London (with my sister Hilary) but also a box of chocolates and a weekend of pampering at Henlow Grange Health Farm.

Susan King, Biggleswade, Beds

Susan and Diane, The Green Goddess, share a toast

Writers' Britain
Ayrshire: Burns' Country

Lovely Lowlands

For fans of the Scottish bard, Robert Burns, January is a special month. The world over, his song Auld Lang Syne is sung on New Year's Eve and his memory is commemorated again on Burns' Night, January 25.

Born in 1759 in Alloway, just south of the town of Ayr, Burns died, aged 37, in Dumfries. Spurning the attractions of big cities like Edinburgh or Glasgow, he spent most of his short life in the rugged countryside of Ayrshire and Dumfries & Galloway which inspired much of his poetry.

The Burns Heritage Trail takes tourists on a circular tour of south west Scotland that includes visitor centres, museums and statues, all celebrating the great man's life and works. The simple cottage where he was born still stands, as do several of his later homes and the inns he loved to frequent, many preserved in their original state. Among the latter is the Selkirk Arms where Burns recited the famous Selkirk Grace.

> *Some hae meat and canna eat,*
> *And some wad eat that want it;*
> *But we hae meat, and we can eat,*
> *Sae let the Lord be thankit.*

Another of Burns' best loved poems is recreated by the Tam O'Shanter Experience which is situated within the Burns National Heritage Park.

Other attractions of this area include country walks in the Carrick Hills or the Galloway Forest Park as well as many good golf courses. For shoppers, the 100-year-old Waverley Mill in Selkirk offers the chance to buy tweeds and a range of tartans, including the Diana Princess of Wales Memorial Tartan.

PIC: VISITSCOTLAND DUMFRIES & GALLOWAY

Home from the sea

A fine romance

Mrs Lilian Roberts of Whitby found that first impressions can be wrong

In 1947 I was 18, living with my Mother and Father in the small village of South Hylton near Durham. I was a shy 'country bumpkin' who just quietly made the sandwiches for Mum and Dad and their friends when they returned from their Saturday evening sing-song at the Golden Lion pub.

My cousin Dahlia and her sailor husband were one of the crowd and they had brought along a pal of his, Taff Roberts. This Taff was 23, a big, brash Welshman. Mind you, he had lovely eyes and dark brown curly hair but I thought he was a bit full of himself. (We later learned that he had joined the Navy when he was only 15 and his ship had been torpedoed two years after that.)

The next day they called round to ask if I would make a foursome to go to the pictures. I was rather embarrassed as I was wearing a turban over my curling pins and my eyes and nose were red from peeling onions.

I decided to go along and we had a good time, but Taff's leave was up and away he went to Scotland. Hugh (his real name) wrote to me as soon as he got back to his base, thanking my family for their hospitality. Soon he started writing just to me.

He came to spend Christmas with us and at Easter he took me home to Anglesey to meet his mum. We were married in August 1948.

In 60 years of marriage there has never been a dull moment. We have travelled the world together, had four children and nine grandchildren, and our love is as strong now as it has ever been.

What's in a name?

Many of our favourite stars were originally known by another name. Match the star to their birth name. If you get stuck the answers are at the bottom of the page

PIC: REX FEATURES

1.	Billie Holiday	A.	Arnold George Dorsey
2.	Bob Hope	B.	Arthur Stanley Jefferson
3.	Engelbert Humperdink	C.	Burton Stephen Lancaster
4.	Elton John	D.	Constance Frances Marie Ockelman
5.	Vivien Leigh	E.	Dino Paul Crocetti
6.	Boris Karloff	F.	Eleanora Fagan
7.	Gene Kelly	G.	Eugene Curran Kelly
8.	Veronica Lake	H.	Friedrich Robert Donath
9.	Burt Lancaster	I.	Hedwig Eva Maria Kiesler
10.	Stan Laurel	J.	Jeanette Helen Morrison
11.	Peggy Lee	K.	Leslie Hornby
12.	Janet Leigh	L.	Leslie Townes Hope
13.	Sophia Loren	M.	Marion Michael Morrison
14.	Jayne Mansfield	N.	Norma Dolores Engstrom
15.	Dean Martin	O.	Reginald Kenneth Dwight
16.	Ringo Starr	P.	Richard Henry Sellers
17.	Twiggy	Q.	Richard Starkey
18.	John Wayne	R.	Sofia Villani Scicolone
19.	Hedy Lamarr	S.	Vera Jayne Palmer
20.	Robert Donat	T.	Vivian Mary Hartley
21.	Peter Sellers	U.	William Henry Pratt

Answers: 1F, 2L, 3A, 4O, 5T, 6U, 7G, 8D, 9C, 10B, 11N, 12J, 13R, 14S, 15E, 16Q, 17K, 18M, 19I, 20H, 21P

Quilts aren't cool

BY: VALERIE BOWES

How can Justine hide her gran's well-meant gift?

Justine wailed: "Mum! No! Can't you stop her?" Her mother replied: "How can I? You know Nanna loves making patchwork quilts."

Justine scowled. She was sure her friend Kayla would fall about laughing if she saw a home-made quilt on Justine's bed. And Justine would prefer a slow death to incurring Kayla's disapproval.

"Nanna's making it specially for you. None of your friends will have anything like it."

"Too right," Justine said with bitter emphasis. "I bet it'll be all pastel blues and pinks. Mum, you've got to stop her."

But she knew there was no hope of that. Nanna saved every old garment, every scrap of material. She could tell you where each patch came from and what had happened while it was still a skirt or a curtain or whatever. 'Making memories', Nanna called it.

'She thinks I'm still five, not thirteen', Justine thought despairingly. 'I'll have to tell her I don't want it'. But how could she do that without hurting Nanna's feelings?

The brown paper package was waiting for her when she got home from school a couple of days later. And it was just as bad as she'd feared. Neat rows of girlie pink and sunshine yellow squares interspersed with a cute little teddy-bear print. Yuk!

Justine gazed at it in horror. She couldn't put that on her bed. Kayla would laugh herself silly and then tell everyone at school. Justine felt her face burn at the very thought.

"Isn't it lovely!" her mum said, smoothing it with a gentle hand.

"It's awful! You have it, if you like it so much."

"I've got one, thanks," Mum reminded her, "and Nanna will be so upset if she thinks you don't like it."

Justine kicked the bedleg, moodily. What was she going to do? She loved her Nanna, but she didn't want this childish gift.

For several days, she made excuses to go round to Kayla's home instead of having her friend come to hers – but that wasn't going to work forever.

Then Justine had her idea.

"I'm taking that quilt to school," she announced. "I told Mrs Cartwright about it and she wants to see it."

"Well, be careful with it. Nanna's coming this afternoon, don't forget."

Justine bundled the quilt into a bag and set off. Her plan was to 'accidentally' leave it on the train but it wasn't as easy as she'd thought. When she got up as her station approached, a woman call out after her: "You've forgotten your parcel!"

Justine snatched up the package without a word

She had to find somewhere to dump it

and flounced off the train. She heard the woman say indignantly: "Well! Don't they teach them manners, these days?"

Her next idea was to stick it in the waste bin. But the only bin she could find was already overflowing with rubbish. No matter. She'd leave the quilt beside it.

"Hoy!" bellowed the station porter. "Can't you read?" He pointed at a notice warning people to take all their belongings with them. "Want to cause a major incident, do you? Close the line while we get the bomb squad in to check that out?"

"Oh, right, I always carry bombs about," Justine retorted sarcastically. "It's rubbish. I don't want it."

"Well, put it in your own bin," the man snapped. "You can't leave it there."

Justine looked around desperately as she walked along. She had to find somewhere to dump it before she reached school, otherwise Kayla would want to know what it was. A row of wheelie bins outside a shop caught her eye. Perfect!

She sidled up to them. These bins were full, too,

As the day wore on, she fell prey to feelings of guilt

ILLUSTRATION: KATE DAVIES

so she squashed the bag down behind them and scuttled off quickly.

But as the day wore on, she fell prey to feelings of guilt. She couldn't stop thinking of Nanna's kind face, and how much love had gone into making that quilt.

In the middle of a maths lesson, the perfect answer dawned on her. It was so simple. She could put the quilt on her bed when Nanna came, and take it off when Kayla did.

But would the abandoned quilt still be where she'd left it? Visions of the package being lobbed carelessly into the back of a dustcart tormented her for the rest of the day.

As soon as school ended, Justine raced off. Her heart pounded as she saw the bins still standing in a row, and she felt sick with relief when her searching

fingers found the parcel still stuffed behind them.

When she arrived home, Mum and Nanna were enjoying a cup of tea.

"Ah, here she is!" Nanna said fondly, holding out her arms for a hug. "Now, about that quilt I gave you..."

Had Mum told Nanna how much she hated it? Justine squirmed with embarrassment.

Nanna hauled out another brown paper parcel and thrust it into her hands. "Your silly old Nan got her labels mixed up, love. You've got the quilt I made for your little cousin Alice. This is the one I made for you."

With a great effort, Justine pinned a pleased smile onto her face and fumbled the package open.

Swirling patterns. Vibrant, funky colours. Not a cute teddy bear in sight.

"Nanna, that is so cool!" Justine gasped.

She just couldn't wait to show Kayla.

February 2009

Sunday
1

Monday
2

Tuesday
3

Wednesday
4

Thursday
5

Friday
6

Saturday
7

Sunday
8

Monday
9

Tuesday
10

Wednesday
11

Thursday
12

Friday
13

Saturday
14

Valentine's Day

Sunday
15

Monday
16

Tuesday
17

Wednesday
18

Thursday
19

Friday
20

Saturday
21

Sunday
22

Monday	Thursday
23	**26**
Tuesday	Friday
24	**27**
Shrove Tuesday	
Wednesday	Saturday
25	**28**
Ash Wednesday	

Behind the Scenes

Operation Petticoat, 1959

There's a lot of hanging around involved when a film's being made, and the 1959 comedy Operation Petticoat was obviously no exception. The photographer's caught one of its stars, Cary Grant, looking a bit hot and bored – glancing over to see when he's next going to be needed, perhaps?

No lack of laughs in the film, though, as the handsome 55-year-old Cary and co-star Tony Curtis (who was 34 at the time the film was made) take a group of stranded Army nurses on board their submarine. Can it get any worse?

You bet! Having to leave dock in the world's only pink submarine (you'll have to re-acquaint yourselves with the film to find out why) is a huge source of embarrassment for Lt Cmdr Matt Sherman (Grant).

When the film came out, there were probably many young ladies who wished that they were stranded in the tight confines of a submarine with the handsome Mr Grant and Mr Curtis…

PIC: REX FEATURES

Schooldays remembered

Pink custard was my favourite at junior school dinners, but I didn't care too much for the prunes that went with it. There was never any question of leaving anything on our plates, though we ate what was put in front of us, in silence.

Our meals were accompanied by a glass of water poured from huge enamel jugs, and we all wore bib aprons that had our names embroidered by our mothers on the front. It was a different case when I went to secondary school – more a free for all in a noisy hall!

Sylvia Monk, Saffron Walden, Essex

My Grandparents

I have a strong memory of when I was five or six (around 1937), and two of my cousins and I had been left in Grandfather's charge.

I remember sitting on a stool, worrying that Granddad was going to 'tell Mum on me' when she got back and that she'd give me a good hiding. And I was thinking he meant it.

I remember thinking it wasn't fair and that it was Leslie and Ronnie who told me to do it. Ronnie told me he always lit the gas mantels in the house when it got dark, and they called me a coward. I told them I wasn't allowed but they double-dared me.

I got a spill from the box, and stretched over the fireguard to light it from the fire, then I reached up to turn the gas on, but I couldn't reach the knob, so we got a chair, and I stood on it. And that's when the mantelpiece thing (the fringe of velvet material with tassels on it) went 'whoosh', with really big flames.

I didn't scream or do anything, and Ronnie ran in to Granddad, who came running into the room – I didn't think he could run that fast. And he pulled the thing off the mantelpiece and clapped it together with his hands – his hands were really big – and pieces of flame fell from it, up in the air, then on the floor, and Granddad stamped on them, then it was out.

I didn't get a good hiding, just a serious talking-to from my Mother, but I think my Grandfather's threats are what makes this memory so clear to me.

Iris Fisher, Maidstone, Kent

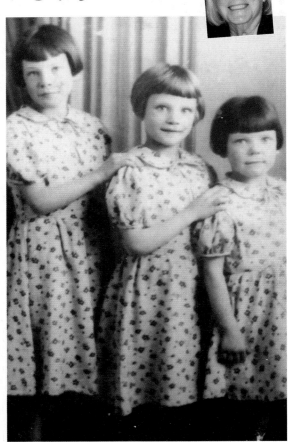

Little Iris (right) with her sisters

Cookery for you

TERIYAKI BEEF SKEWERS WITH ORIENTAL SALSA

Serves 4

450 g (1 lb) lean beef rump or sirloin steaks, cubed
◆ 2 cloves garlic, crushed
◆ 2 cm (³/₄ in) root ginger, peeled and grated
◆ 2 tablespoons each honey and soy sauce
◆ 1 medium red chilli, seeded and chopped
◆ 1 teaspoon sesame seeds
For the oriental salsa
◆ 2 spring onions, thinly sliced
◆ ¹/₂ cucumber, cut into thin strips
◆ 1 medium red chilli, seeded and chopped
◆ 1 tablespoon each soy sauce and sesame oil
◆ 1 teaspoon sesame seeds

1 Mix together the garlic, root ginger, honey, soy sauce, red chilli and sesame seeds. Pour over the beef and mix well to coat.

2 Cover and refrigerate for 2-3 hours, to let the flavours infuse.

3 Preheat barbecue or grill to a medium heat. Thread the cubes onto skewers and cook for 12-15 minutes turning once or twice.

For the oriental salsa

4 Mix together the spring onions, cucumber, red chilli, soy sauce, sesame oil and sesame seeds. Serve with the beef skewers.

Recipe courtesy www.meatmatters.com

Colourful climbers
Clematis cartmanii 'Joe'

Few clematis are as showy as C cartmanii 'Joe', which produces an abundance of small white flowers during late winter – these cover the plant so heavily that the leaves are almost hidden. Like its early-flowering relatives, it benefits from a sheltered position, so choose a sunny corner and let it work its magic! Pruning is not necessary, except to remove straying stems. Height 3m.
Plants widely available.

TOP TIP

When you can't squeeze any more out of your toothpaste tube, cut the end off about 2–3 inches below the opening for a few days' more use. Seal the cut end with a paper clip to keep moist.
Bernice E White, Wantage, Oxon

Healthier for longer!

Drink milk – sip your way through two or more glasses of skimmed milk a day and you could reduce your risk of high blood pressure by up to 10 per cent and strengthen your bones. Milk is packed full of heart healthy calcium, potassium and vitamin D.

THAT'S INTERESTING...

The day most likely to be taken off as sick leave is the first Monday in February.

Cookery for you

CHOCOLATE CHERRY TRIFLE

Serves 4

- ◆ 110g (4oz) good quality dark chocolate
- ◆ 400 ml (14 fl oz) Gold Top milk
- ◆ 3 medium egg yolks
- ◆ 2 tablespoons caster sugar
- ◆ 4 level teaspoons cornflour
- ◆ 1/2 teaspoon vanilla extract
- ◆ 150 g (5 oz) marble cake, broken into chunks
- ◆ 5 tablespoons cherry brandy
- ◆ 8 tablespoons cherry compote
- ◆ 284 ml (1/2 pint) double cream
- ◆ A few fresh cherries, to decorate

1. Chop 1/3 of the chocolate into shards, set aside for decoration.
2. Gently simmer the milk and rest of chocolate in a saucepan, stirring occasionally until the chocolate has melted and the milk has nearly boiled.
3. Whisk the egg yolks, sugar, cornflour and vanilla in a bowl. Then pour in the warm milk, stir well, then put back into the saucepan.
4. Cook on a low heat, stirring to make a smooth, thick custard. Then pour into a clean bowl and leave to cool.
5. Place the cake on the bottom of a trifle bowl. Sprinkle brandy over, then spoon in the compote. Spread the custard on top.
6. Whip the cream until it forms soft peaks and spoon onto the custard.
7. Decorate with chocolate shards and cherries, then serve.

Recipe courtesy Gold Top milk, www.gold-top.co.uk

Colourful climbers
Chaenomeles speciosa

Chaenomeles may not be classed as climbers, but they're fast-growing and can be trained up walls if given support. They're great in early spring because they produce vibrant flowers when little else has emerged, followed by ornamental quince fruits in autumn. Several varieties have awards of Garden Merit from the Royal Horticultural Society and all will easily reach a metre when encouraged up a wall using trellis. Plants widely available.

My Grandparents

Elizabeth's Granny

I had a special relationship with Granny and spent many happy hours with her. Living nearby as a child, I would often cycle to see her on a Sunday and hope she would invite me for tea, as she baked the most delicious meat patties. She was also a good seamstress and made me many pretty dresses – I loved her dearly.

Elizabeth Stiles, Norwich, Norfolk

TOP TIP

If you can't find your windscreen scraper on a cold morning, dig out a plastic card you don't use any more.

Schooldays remembered

Barbara (front row, 4th from left), next to her friend, Helen, in 1950

'Get ready to duck'. It was 1950 and I was in the top class of Addingham High Council School. The headmaster, and our teacher, was Mr Lemon who'd been at the school so long that he'd taught most of the pupils' parents.

We had to write with horrible dip-in pens with scratchy nibs. Anthony was a very messy writer and his sum book was covered in blots, so he was made to use a small blackboard and chalk from the infants' class.

When we took our work up to mark, if we'd made a mistake, Mr Lemon would hurl the book across the classroom. Unfortunately, Anthony usually did something wrong and so when he took his work up we all prepared to duck to avoid being hit by his little blackboard.

My friend, Helen Bolton, and I were lucky because we were monitors. We filled the inkwells and before we had art, we prepared the classroom. Instead of going out to play after lunch, we'd mix the powder paint, then after the lesson we'd wash the paint pots and brushes – we could usually make this last so we missed the last lesson of the afternoon.

Barbara Cox, Hexham, Northumberland

Healthier for longer!

Write a love letter – committing your feelings for your loved ones to paper could help to significantly lower your cholesterol levels and help you avoid future heart problems say researchers at Arizona State University – they have no idea why – but it works!

Meeting the stars

I was 16 in 1959, and three of my friends and I went to Blackpool on holiday. We stayed in a boarding house opposite the Odeon cinema on the north shore. Cliff Richard and the Drifters were on that week, with a full supporting cast, so we couldn't wait to see them.

We had photos taken with Cliff, and Peter Elliott (who'd been on Oh Boy). We also bumped into Edmund Hockridge on the promenade and I had my photo taken with him, too.

Dorothy Lenagan, Wigan, Lancs

Dorothy with Cliff in 1959

Cookery for you

Colourful climbers
Camellia

Producing waxy blooms in a wide range of colours and glossy evergreen leaves, camellias are one of the showiest plants in the spring garden. Since they need shelter to thrive, they respond well to being trained up walls and will put on a colourful display early in the season. A west-facing aspect is ideal as the morning sun may cause frosted flower buds to brown. Camellias prefer neutral or acidic well-drained soils and may reach several metres in height. Plants widely available.

THAT'S INTERESTING...
Dr Beeching's two transport reports, to reduce the cost of running the UK's railway system (the second of which was published on Feb 16, 1965) led to the closure of a quarter of the rail network, including more than 2,000 local stations. Many towns and villages – and thousands of people in remote rural areas – lost their rail link after the cuts.

OAT BREAD WITH CHEDDAR AND GRAINY MUSTARD
Serves 12

- 175 g (6 oz) rolled oats, plus extra to sprinkle
- 250 g (9 oz) strong brown bread flour
- 7 g (½ oz) sachet easy-blend dried yeast
- 1 teaspoon celery salt
- 75g (3 oz) mature Cheddar cheese, finely grated
- 1 tablespoon grainy mustard, plus 1 teaspoon to brush

1 Blend 110g (4 oz) of the oats in a food processor until finely ground. Put into a bowl, add remaining oats and flour. Stir in the yeast, celery salt and cheese. Mix the mustard with 270 ml (½ pint) tepid water and add. Mix to a soft dough, adding more water if the dough feels dry.
2 Turn out onto floured surface and knead for 10 minutes. Transfer to a lightly oiled bowl, cover with cling film and leave in a warm place until doubled in size.
4 Preheat oven to 200°C/400°F/Gas Mark 6. Grease a 900 g (2 lb) loaf tin. Punch the dough to deflate and turn out onto the work surface. Shape into an oblong and drop into the tin. Cover with greased cling film and leave in a warm place until the dough fills the tin (about 1 hour).
5 Mix the teaspoon of mustard with 1 teaspoon water and brush over the dough. Scatter with extra oats and bake for 35-40 minutes, until pale golden. Cool on wire rack.

Recipe courtesy www.allaboutoats.com

My Grandparents

This photo of my maternal Grandmother Florence Butler was taken in her twenties. I knew her when she was in her 60s, during the Second World War. We visited her with my mother and aunt Jessie, when I was nine and my sister Valerie, seven.

Nanna Butler lived with Grandfather Stephen, who was confined in wheelchair with rheumatoid arthritis. She was very strict and stern, and kept a cane at the dining room table which was used on knuckles, if hands or elbows were resting on the top during a meal.

I'm afraid I did something wrong one weekend, accidentally kicking some pots in the hearth. I was reprimanded but my mother stuck up for me, and the outcome was we were evicted late on a Sunday afternoon.

As we trudged up the high street to the railway station with our luggage, a local woman called out that there were no trains until the next morning, but we could stay the night with her.

The four of us shared a double bed and, to our horror, with a lot of bedbugs! We survived the night, but Aunt Jessie realised she'd left her wristwatch at Grandma's and I was sent to retrieve it. I was told to say that if Grandma asked where we slept, I was to say, a field. All was forgiven later…

Olive Barker, Waltham Abbey, Essex

Florence Butler

Schooldays remembered

Valerie (3rd row from the front, 4th from right) and her classmates

My first school was The Green C of E School, Tottenham, and I remember the school dinners. They were brought in from outside because we had no canteen, so by the time it was lunch break, the cabbage was soggy and the school reeked of it. I just hated school dinners and used to stuff my pockets with food, or drop it under the table.

Valerie Temple, Great Dunmow, Essex

Cookery for you

CARAMEL PECAN PANCAKES

Serves 4–6

- ◆ 8 ready-made dessert pancakes
- ◆ 25 g (1 oz) butter, for greasing
- ◆ 55 g (2 oz) pecans, lightly toasted
- ◆ 1 large orange, grated zest and juice
- ◆ 1 tablespoon caster sugar
- ◆ 8 tablespoons Carnation Caramel

1 Preheat grill to medium, or oven to 200°C/ 400°F/ Gas Mark 6.
2 Lightly butter a shallow ovenproof dish. Fold the pancakes into eighths and arrange in the dish. Scatter over the pecans, orange zest and juice. Sprinkle over the caster sugar.
3 Place in the grill or oven for 5 minutes, or until the pancakes are heated through and the edges are crispy.
4 Remove from the heat and pour over the Carnation Caramel. Serve at once.

Recipe courtesy Nestlé Carnation, www.carnation.co.uk

TOP TIP

For a natural, sweet smelling room, put a few drops of fragrance oil in the water containers hanging from your radiators. **Ethel Corduff, London SE25**

My Grandparents

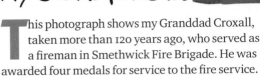

This photograph shows my Granddad Croxall, taken more than 120 years ago, who served as a fireman in Smethwick Fire Brigade. He was awarded four medals for service to the fire service.

Norman Leavesley, Halesowen, W Mids

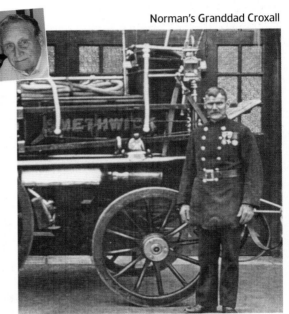

Norman's Granddad Croxall

Healthier for longer!

Take a nap – it could improve your memory, according to a study in the journal Sleep. All you need is a 45 minute snooze during the day to boost your grey matter.

■ THAT'S INTERESTING...

The carrot originated around 5,000 years ago in Middle Asia around Afghanistan, and slowly spread into the Mediterranean area. The first carrots were white, purple, red, yellow/green and black – not orange. Today, there is a different carrot variety for every letter of the alphabet.

Schooldays remembered

Eve in 1952

I went to a boarding school in Slough in the early 1950s and remember night times in the dormitory after lights out. There was a row of beds either side with a bath-cum-washroom nearby. We made lots of noise while undressing and washing and, when we were in our pyjamas, the duty teacher would say, 'into bed now girls'. The routine was that we were given five minutes to settle down, and then 'lights out', and that's when the fun began.

The teacher would tour the dormitories every quarter of an hour, so we had time to play 'dare'. A favourite was to swap beds just before the teacher passed through again, and we would make a slight noise so that she might put the light on. Would she notice? Sometimes, and punishments could follow. The most terrifying time was standing outside on the windowsill outside the dormitory on the first floor.

One night we'd decided on Cowboys and Indians (before PC) and I had been captured and tied to the end of my bed. The teacher came in early and bumped into me as she passed through the dark room. The lights went on, and everyone pretended to be asleep. 'Still got lots of energy, girls? Let's make use of it'. And she got everyone to strip their beds and turn the mattress – not once but twice. We didn't move a muscle once we got back into bed.

Eve Sinfield, Brighton, E Sussex

Colourful climbers

Clematis cartmanii 'Avalanche'

O ne of the earliest clematis to flower, C cartmanii 'Avalanche' is one New Zealand hybrid that was well worth importing. Unlike the leaves of many varieties, its foliage is extremely pretty and makes an attractive backdrop for the white flowers which smother it during the spring. It's borderline hardy so is best planted in a container, sheltered garden or cool greenhouse, where it may reach 1.8m in height. Plants widely available.

Meeting the stars

I've been an Adam Faith fan most of my life. I first saw him in pantomime at Wimbledon Theatre in 1960 with my parents, and I was hooked. Over the years I watched him on television and saw him 'live' whenever I could.

In 1994 I saw him in Alfie at Richmond Theatre. After the show, we joined the crowd at the Stage Door, and it wasn't very long before he appeared – I almost fainted in anticipation! I met him several times after that, and each time he was always the same – natural and unaffected, the perfect gentleman.

I once bumped into him in Hampstead, and chatted to him while he collected his dry cleaning – and here's the photo.

I still miss him and wish they would repeat his series, Love Hurts, again.

Janice Stocker, Mitcham, Surrey

Janice and Adam in 1995

Yorkshire: Brontë Country

Windswept Heights

Any tour of Brontë Country must centre on Haworth and its world famous parsonage. First opened as a museum in 1928, Haworth Parsonage was home to the three Brontë sisters, their brother Branwell, and their father who was the rector of the adjacent church. It was here that Charlotte wrote Jane Eyre and Emily penned Wuthering Heights.

After exploring the steep streets, quaint shops and tearooms of the hilltop town, visitors can set forth on walks across the Pennine moors to discover the isolated farmstead of Top Withens, said to be the inspiration for Wuthering Heights, and a local beauty spot known as the Brontë waterfall.

The family moved to Haworth in 1820 from Thornton, near Bradford, where all four of the children were born. The house in Market Street is marked by a plaque on the wall giving their dates of birth. Apart from Anne, all of the Brontës are buried in Haworth. Anne's grave is to be found in the seaside resort of Scarborough in St Mary's churchyard on Castle Hill.

Further afield, near to Ingleton in the Yorkshire Dales, is the village of Cowan Bridge where the school is said to be the original of the dreadful Lowood School attended by Jane Eyre. In 1833, the Brontë family went on an excursion to the lovely remains of Bolton Abbey, which continue to attract many visitors to the area.

Other attractions include the Keighley and Worth Valley Railway which runs from Haworth to the village of Oxenhope and is known to many film buffs for its central role in The Railway Children.

Rough and tumble

Ah! Happy days

Tony Crump of Nottingham was one of the gang

My Mam's house in a large Midlands city has gone now, replaced by a children's playground, but whenever I pass by the memories come flooding back.

I remember the sound of the dray-horses' hooves on cobblestones as the barrels of beer were unloaded at the off-licence next door. Each wooden barrel rolled off the cart with a muffled thud onto a bed of sacks on the pavement. The caretaker from the church hall across the road used to rush out collect the piles of horse manure for his roses.

We didn't have a garden as ours was a back-to-back house with outside toilets and a single cold tap in the kitchen sink. The kitchen was always referred to as the scullery. It had a copper boiler built into one corner with a fire grate beneath it to heat the water.

Washdays, particularly in winter, were a nightmare. I remember the products we used: ACDO soap powder and little packets of Reckitt's starch. We all took turns winding the handle of the mangle, then watched Mam do the ironing with an iron heated on the gas stove,

its handle wrapped in a rag to prevent burns.

In those days, we lads went around in gangs. We were just as boisterous as today's kids but we had more respect for authority. Our gang met in the stables which backed on to our yard and we spent hours up in the loft planning raids on rival gangs.

Bloodthirsty as the planning was, with dire threats of retribution, in reality we lived in peaceful co-existence with the Leen Gang and the Green Gang. We merely fantasised, then avoided each other.

The handmaiden's story

It's all very well being on stage at the Royal Opera House, but quite another if you can't see where you're going, as Clare Shortt discovered...

It was 1964, and Maria Callas and Tito Gobbi were to appear at Covent Garden in Tosca. I was a young actress with not much work and very little money.

I wasn't really interested in opera as an art form, but the desire to see these two great stars was overwhelming. Tickets at Covent Garden were beyond my means but I'd heard that out of work actors and actresses were used as walk-ons. I knew there was a long processional scene in Tosca so I wrote to the theatre and suggested that I might be suitable.

Some days later, much to my surprise, I was invited to meet the lady in charge of the' supernumeraries', as I found out they were called. Tosca was going to be possible after all!

It was quite a meeting – and Stella was delightful, treating me as if I were the star. She showed me round the theatre, explained the supernumerary system, introduced me to whoever we met on our tour but told me that the extras for Tosca had already been contacted. By way of consolation she promised to be in touch for future operas.

After all her kindness I didn't feel I could say I wasn't interested in other operas.

But Stella wasn't to be denied. A few weeks later the telephone rang. Could I present myself at the theatre that evening? It had

Clare in her handmaiden days!

been explained to me at that first meeting that they always had an 'extra extra' just in case of a disaster. The extra extra was not required to go on stage but watch the performance so they would know what to do when required. And that was what I was to do that evening, and be paid two guineas. The opera was Aida.

I arrived at the theatre and took my place at the side of the stage. I'd not been settled very long when I saw a worried Stella approaching. One of the princess's handmaidens hadn't arrived and I was to take her place.

It was presumed I had a working knowledge of the opera as it was a production that had been in repertoire for some considerable time. However, I was told that it was quite an easy role

and the chief handmaiden would tell me what to do.

What I wasn't told was the costume had a headpiece that obscured my peripheral vision entirely. I was instructed by the chief handmaiden to, 'Follow me. Walk up the steps at the centre of the stage, come to rest on the third step from the top, stand stage left of me and kneel just before I do'.

As I'd no idea how long I was to stand on the steps and my headdress prevented me from seeing when she knelt I didn't see how I could kneel either before or after her!

Nevertheless follow her I did, stand on the steps I did, while the Grand March from Aida filled that magnificent theatre and transformed even the most reluctant handmaiden into a thrilled and excited participant.

To stand on that great stage and watch the seemingly unending column of soldiers march across was quite breathtaking. A Covent Garden enthusiast was born.

Other operas followed until the return of Tosca. So I eventually got my wish. I took part in the procession to the church of Sant'Andrea della Valle in Act One and was allowed to stand in the wings for the remainder of the opera and enjoy Maria Callas and Tito Gobbi's magnificent interpretation of Puccini's music.

March 2009

Sunday **1** <div align="right">St David's Day</div>	Thursday **12**
Monday **2**	Friday **13**
Tuesday **3**	Saturday **14**
Wednesday **4**	Sunday **15**
Thursday **5** <div align="right">Crufts begins</div>	Monday **16**
Friday **6**	Tuesday **17** <div align="right">St Patrick's Day (Bank Holiday, N Ireland)</div>
Saturday **7**	Wednesday **18**
Sunday **8**	Thursday **19**
Monday **9** <div align="right">Commonwealth Day</div>	Friday **20**
Tuesday **10**	Saturday **21**
Wednesday **11** <div align="right">National No Smoking Day</div>	Sunday **22** <div align="right">Mothering Sunday</div>

Monday
23

Tuesday
24

Wednesday
25

Thursday
26

Friday
27

Saturday
28

Sunday
29

British Summer Time (BST) begins
Oxford/Cambridge Boat Race

Monday
30

Tuesday
31

PIC: REX FEATURES

Behind the Scenes

Marnie, 1964

It must be pleasant to earn a living lying in bed, but someone's got to do it…

Here's 'Tippi' Hedren, who looks comfortable as she takes direction from Sir Alfred Hitchcock, during the making of the psychological thriller Marnie, in 1964. Sean Connery, and Diane Baker (who plays Connery's sister-in-law in the film) look on.

The film was adapted from a Winston Graham novel, about a paranoid young woman (played by Tippi) who is a compulsive thief, and who must face her troubled past to rid herself of her behaviour. Sean Connery plays Mark Rutland, the man who eventually becomes her husband – but there's no happy honeymoon for the newlyweds.

Tippi, who is Melanie Griffiths' mother, was well known as a model when discovered by Hitchcock, who also cast her in his film, The Birds. Sean Connery had already made his first outing as James Bond two years before, in Dr No.

Schooldays remembered

I went to a small C of E Primary School which had separate boys and girls' playgrounds, with a high wall between – which just had to be climbed so we could sit on the top and jeer at each other.

The toilets were outside and very cold in winter, and in the summer the more advanced pupils used them for snogging.

As a small child, I loved the huge rocking horse in the infants' classroom and the Janet and John story books. I hated steak and kidney pudding, and swede. The head cook was very strict and many lunch breaks found me tearfully chewing cold steak and kidney pudding while my classmates were outside playing.

Spelling tests were easy, chanting multiplication tables not so good. I became a milk monitor so that I didn't have to give myself warm bottles of milk, which I hated!

The school enforced strict discipline and my

Christine and her brother Ray in 1964

brother often fell foul of the rules – self-satisfied children would say to me at playtime, 'Your brother's waiting outside the headmaster's study again'.

Christine Barrett, Bournemouth, Dorset

My Grandparents

Below: Charles and Emma Rogers

My grandparents, Charles and Emma Rogers lived in a small terraced house in North End Road in Hampstead, London, occupying two rooms on the first floor. All the tenants shared a toilet on the landing and there was no bathroom. Between 1892 and 1914, they had nine daughters, all brought up in the two rooms.

Grandfather served in the old 3rd Middlesex Rifles and took part in the parade past Queen Victoria in the Jubilee Celebrations at Buckingham Palace in 1887.

When my grandparents celebrated their golden wedding, my grandfather told the local reporter that he'd been a waggoner, a railway navvy and a gravedigger and didn't retire until he was 70.

Their one simple pleasure was to go to the famous pub The Old Bull and Bush for a drink on a Saturday night. On one occasion the local paper reported a court case involving two men worse for drink, insulting the barmaid and starting fighting. The

barmaid appealed for help and grandfather firmly ejected them; he was highly praised by the police and the local magistrate.

Sadly, he died before I reached an age where I could have talked to him about his life. Fortunately, my cousins and I were able to enjoy many more years with our dear grandmother. We often took her for a cup of tea and a bun in a Lyons Teashop.

Gordon Carter, York, North Yorks

Cookery for you

BAKED SEA BASS WITH TENDERSTEM® BROCCOLI AND NEW POTATOES

Serves 4

- ◆ 800 g (1 lb 10 oz) new potatoes, halved lengthways
For the seabass
- ◆ 4 x 350 g (12 oz) whole sea bass, scaled and gutted
- ◆ 4 tablespoons olive oil
- ◆ 300 g (11 oz) Tenderstem® broccoli
- ◆ 50 g (2 oz) unsalted butter
- ◆ 1 clove garlic, finely chopped
- ◆ 4 anchovy fillets chopped
- ◆ Small bunch parsley, shredded
- ◆ 1 lemon cut into quarters

1 Preheat oven to 220°C/425°F/Gas Mark 7.
2 Score the skin of the sea bass, rub with olive oil and season. Place on a non-stick baking tray and place in the oven for 15 minutes. The fish is cooked when the flesh easily comes away from the bone.
3 Meanwhile boil the new potatoes until cooked.
4 When the potatoes and sea bass are cooked, leave in a warm place. Boil the broccoli till just cooked.
5 Divide the fish, potatoes and broccoli between 4 plates.
6 In a small saucepan, heat the butter until it starts to brown, add the garlic and anchovies and cook for 30 seconds. Stir in the parsley and some pepper.
7 Pour the butter over the fish, potatoes and broccoli and serve with a wedge of lemon.

Recipe courtesy Tenderstem® broccoli www.tenderstem.co.uk

Colourful climbers
Fan-trained plums, damsons and gages

One of the earliest groups of trees to flower in spring are the plums, damsons and gages and their blossom is extremely attractive. They may not be climbers but they fruit best when trained up against a sunny south-facing wall. They thrive in well-drained soils but prefer those that remain moist. Most, such as 'Goldfinch', are self-fertile, so only one is needed for successful fruiting. Netting may be necessary to protect the crop. Plants widely available.

TOP TIP
If your soap always sticks to the soap dish, rub a little petroleum jelly onto the dish.

Healthier for longer!

Sip beetroot juice – just 500ml a day could significantly reduce your blood pressure say researchers at The London School of Medicine. Within an hour the special dietary nitrates found in beetroot juice get to work bringing your blood pressure down.

THAT'S INTERESTING...
The Brown Hare is the fastest land mammal in the UK, reaching speeds of up to 45mph.

Cookery for you

BERRY PANETTONE

Serves 6

- ◆ 450 g (1 lb) mixed berries, such as strawberries, raspberries and blueberries
- ◆ 100 ml (3¹/₂ fl oz) sweet dessert wine
- ◆ 100 g (3¹/₂ oz) caster sugar
- ◆ 3 mini panettone
- ◆ 397 g can of Carnation Chocolate filling
- ◆ Cocoa for dusting, optional

1 Put the berries into a bowl, halving or quartering any large strawberries. Mix together the wine and sugar and pour over the fruit. Leave to chill for an hour, stirring occasionally.

2 Cut off the rounded top of each panettone and slice the rest into quarters. Lightly toast the slices until golden brown.

3 To serve, place a slice of panettone onto individual serving plates. Drizzle some Carnation chocolate filling on top and then spoon over the fruit mixture. Top with a second slice, more chocolate filling and fruit. Dust with a little cocoa and serve.

Tips: You can also make this dessert in one dish or replace the mixed berries with orange segments, sliced mango and banana.

Recipe courtesy Nestlé Carnation, www.carnation.co.uk

My Grandparents

My beloved Grannie was born on the Blenheim Palace Estate in 1873, where her parents worked. Grannie had three sisters and six brothers, and one, George, went to work at Cadbury as a supervisor.

Grannie and her sisters never had an education, and she could neither read nor write; she went to work in a convent at nine years old, later joining her sisters at Cadbury.

When she married, she came to live in Rugeley, Staffs. She had a hard life, never seeing Granddad's wages half the time, but she managed to get to Birmingham now and then to visit her sisters.

On one occasion, she'd taken my mother on the train, and when it was time to leave, the family packed a basket full of goodies and food for her. She hadn't gone far when a car drew up, and it was Mr Cadbury.

"Hello, Sally," he said, "How are you? I haven't seen you for a while". She told him she'd been visiting the family

Sarah Elizabeth Mountford, on her 18th birthday in 1891

and was walking to the station to catch the train to Rugeley.

"We can't have you walking with that heavy basket, and the little one looks tired." (Mum was five.)

He drove them to the station and when they arrived, a photographer took a picture of them all in the car. Mr Cadbury took them to the platform, shook Grannie's hand and said he hoped to see them again.

A couple of weeks later a photograph of her with Mr Cadbury arrived, and she treasured it all her life. Sadly, it was lost when she died.

**Dee Bushnell,
Rugeley, Staffs**

THAT'S INTERESTING...

The fear of Friday the 13th is called paraskavedekatriaphobia.

Schooldays remembered

Jan - with not a fox in sight!

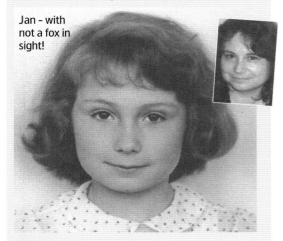

My memories of infants school are of winning a raffle for a stuffed fox in a glass cabinet and at the time feeling so proud that it was me who'd won! Now, my thoughts are the same as my Mum's at the time – she wasn't at all impressed and made me put it in the shed.

**Jan Fearnley,
Littlehampton, W Sussex**

TOP TIP

When greasing a tin or bowl, don't tear off bits of greaseproof, or mutilate your butter wrapper – instead buy a cheap batch of greaseproof cake cases to use when greasing. They are just the right size for your fingers.
Margaret Walker, Porthmadog, Gwynedd

Healthier for longer!

Get moving – it could make you younger from the inside out say UK researchers. We already know that a regular workout helps to reduce your risk of serious health problems such heart disease, diabetes and osteoporosis. But now scientists have found that regular exercise could actually help to slow down your body's ageing process too. Grab those trainers for fewer wrinkles.

Meeting the stars

I started out in 1952 as a sign-writer and gradually started painting portraits. I've always been sport mad, so naturally I painted my heroes, including Bjorn Borg, Geoff Boycott, Frank Bruno, Alex Higgins, Billie Jean King, Jayne Torvill and Christopher Dean, Virginia Wade and Graham Gooch.

Peter Billingham, Bridport, Dorset

Peter with Jayne Torvill and Christopher Dean

Colourful climbers
Clematis alpina 'Ruby'

Unlike its blowsier summer cousins, the alpina species of clematis is more delicate with light green leaves and gently nodding flowers in early spring. Reaching only 3m in height, 'Ruby' is less rampant than many others. Pruning is unnecessary, so let it scramble through the lower branches of a tree or plant it at the base of an east fence or wall and enjoy. Plants widely available.

TOP TIP

If you get ink on a white shirt, rub toothpaste on the stain with a little brush, leave for a minute or two, then rinse. Wash the shirt as normal.

Cookery for you

Colourful climbers

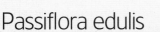

Passiflora edulis

Passiflora edulis is the best and hardiest variety if you want to eat the fruits, and survives happily in sheltered gardens. However, in a heated conservatory it will not only start flowering much earlier – even during March – it's also more likely to produce edible fruits. It grows well inside and will put on several metres of growth. Seed is available from Jungle Seeds at www.jungleseeds.co.uk

THAT'S INTERESTING...

Other names attributed to Mothering Sunday include Simnel Sunday, Refreshment Sunday and Rose Sunday. Simnel Sunday is named after the practice of baking Simnel cakes to celebrate the reuniting of families during the austerity of Lent, when young girls in service would make one to take home to their mothers on their day off.

MUSHROOMS WITH CHEESE, HAM AND OATS
Serves 4

- ◆ 4 large flat Portabello mushrooms
- ◆ 200 g (7 oz) low fat cream cheese
- ◆ 4 spring onions, chopped
- ◆ 110 g (4 oz) ham, diced
- ◆ 25 g (1 oz) oats
- ◆ 2 tablespoons coarse oatmeal

1 Preheat the oven to 200°C/400°F/Gas Mark 6.
2 Make 2 large squares of foil, place 2 mushrooms on each, rounded edge down. Divide the cream cheese between the 4 mushrooms, then sprinkle over the spring onions and ham.
3 Mix together the oats and oatmeal, dry fry in a pan then sprinkle over the mushrooms. Fold over the foil and seal to create a parcel. Place the parcels on a large baking tray and bake for 20 minutes. Great served immediately or cold.

Recipe courtesy www.wholegraingoodness.com

Healthier for longer!

Eat for a healthy heart – and protect your prostate. Eating four or more heart healthy servings of vegetables every day could reduce your risk of an enlarged prostate by 32 per cent and swapping fatty red meats for lean protein could lower your risk by another 15 per cent, say US scientists.

My Grandparents

My Grandmother was born in 1887 and died in 1966. She was a wonderful woman, nearly blind but still made the journey from Edenbridge, Kent to Surrey each week to see us. This meant walking to the station, and catching the steam train to Croydon, then a bus to Wallington.

One day she arrived and said to my mother: "I've brought you some anemone bulbs," and handed them to her in a paper bag. Looking in the bag, my mum said: "These aren't anemone bulbs but brazil nuts." "Oh my goodness," said my Grandmother, "I've eaten the bulbs." Because of her bad eyesight, she'd mistaken them for the brazil nuts. All ended well, though, as the bulbs didn't make her ill.

Audrey Baker, Ringwood, Hants

Grandmother Hilda Humphrey

Schooldays remembered

It was the day of our junior school's annual photograph session and we were to come to school dressed tidily.

I saw my new dress laid out on my bed, which mum must have worked on late into the night to get it ready, so I quickly put it on and went off to school.

The Headmaster told us that Mr Beeman, the photographer, would be taking photos straight after assembly while our uniforms were clean and smart. One by one, we were all 'snapped' then the bell rang for break.

We ran to the top of the playing field to play 'tick and on' with the boys. "Marg! You're on!" shouted Kath. I caught one of the boys, grabbed him by the collar, and in retaliation he grabbed mine and it came away in his hand.

I felt a fool, but carried on playing,

when another, more boisterous lad tackled me like a rugby player and as a result, my dress completely disintegrated, leaving me in navy knickers and white vest. My pals were hysterical but, fortunately, a kind dinner lady had been watching and hurried into the lost property office for some shorts and gave me a bag to put my dress pieces in.

Mum realised straight away what had happened. "The dress was only tacked," she said, "I thought the photo session was tomorrow and I'd put your dress on your bed for you to try on." It was a long time before I lived that one down.

My classmates would tug at the collar of my dresses and say, 'Just testing'.

Margaret Turner, Warrington, Cheshire

Wendy aged 9, dress intact!

Cookery for you

FROZEN VANILLA YOGHURT WITH RASPBERRIES

Serves 4-6

- ◆ 50 g (2 oz) oats
- ◆ 2 x 450 g (1 lb) tubs low fat vanilla yoghurt
- ◆ 150 g (5 oz) tub low fat custard
- ◆ 250 g (9 oz) fresh raspberries, plus extra for serving
- ◆ 2 tablespoons honey
- ◆ Handful of fresh mint leaves

1 Toast the oats in a dry frying pan until golden, then cool.
2 Mix together the yoghurt, custard and oats. Place in a freezer-proof container and freeze for 2 hours.
3 Meanwhile, cook the raspberries and honey in a small saucepan for 5 minutes, or until softened. Allow to cool
4 Stir the raspberries into the yoghurt mixture to create a marbled effect and freeze for a further 2-3 hours.
5 Remove from the freezer and rest for 30 minutes before serving. Sprinkle with the toasted oats and serve with fresh raspberries and mint.

Tips: Try using fresh strawberries instead of raspberries, or use flavoured yoghurts.

Recipe courtesy www.wholegraingoodness.com

My Grandparents

This is a photo of me with my Granddad, Richard Oliver, in 1929, on Polperro Harbour. He was a seaman and sailed around the world many times before retiring and becoming a fisherman. The jersey he is wearing was knitted by my Grandmother (in Cornwall we call them frocks). Each port has a different pattern so, if they were shipwrecked, they would know where the sailor came from.

My Grandmother Mary was a clever woman; when she died she left five houses, one for each of her children. She made some of her money by knitting, the rest by cleaning and gutting fish (pilchards) on the harbour. **Dorothy Aitken, Looe, Cornwall**

Left: Dorothy and Granddad Oliver
Below: Mary and Richard Oliver

TOP TIP

Use an old makeup brush for dusting nooks and crannies.

THAT'S INTERESTING...

Spring cleaning shouldn't just be confined to your house – do the same for your make up. Throw out anything over six months old that you can't wash. It's estimated that 50% of minor eye infections are caused by old eye makeup.

Schooldays remembered

I passed my eleven plus and went to John Leggott Grammar School in Lincolnshire in 1968. Very strange as we had boys in the class, which we hadn't had at junior school.

We made a cookery apron in our first year, then a skirt and blouse which we had to model in a show at the end of the school year.

Susan in grammar school uniform

The next year we did cookery instead but all this entailed was learning how to wash pans, and the only cookery we did was with apples – baked with custard and stewed – and we made jam buns but that was about it.

We always had to wear our brown Juliette caps – part of our brown and cream uniform – until we were home. Our gymslip skirts had to be the correct length; when we knelt down the hem had to reach the floor.

My father was in hospital when I got my first school uniform and I went to see him wearing it as I was so proud and wanted to show it off. Needless to say, I was glad never to have to wear it again when I eventually left school!

Susan Green, Scunthorpe, N Lincs

Healthier for longer!

Get more vitamin E – it could help keep you moving as you get older. Researchers found that people with low levels of vitamin E in their diets were more likely to experience a decline in their physical abilities than people who got plenty from foods such as olive oil, nuts and green leafy vegetables.

Colourful climbers
Kerria japonica

Normally classified as a spring flowering shrub, Kerria japonica will grow almost anywhere, reliably producing a thicket of graceful stems that are covered in lovely yellow flowers. It may not climb but it responds well to being grown against a wall – especially one that faces north because direct sunshine bleaches the flowers. Also, since it suckers, a wall helps keep it within bounds – chop around the base with a spade every year to prevent it becoming invasive. Height 3m. Plants widely available.

Meeting the stars

I first met my idol Marty Wilde in 1960 at Finsbury Park Empire – that's me on the left of the photograph. I was a teenager in love, aged 16. Marty had just married Joyce of the Vernon Girls.

My husband Doug and I have been going to his gigs regularly over the years. Marty's never changed, he always has time to speak and never rushes away.

In 2007 Marty celebrated his 50th year in showbusiness at the London Palladium.

Marilyn Smith, Kelso, Roxburghshire

Marty then... ... and now

South Tyneside: Catherine Cookson Country

Shipyard heritage

Born Katie McMullen in 1906, Catherine Cookson left her native Tyneside at the age of 22. She didn't start writing until she was in her forties but many of her most powerful novels are set in the area where she grew up, which was then known as County Durham.

Catherine's earliest home was 5 Leam Lane, Tyne Dock in what is now South Shields. When she was five, the family moved to William Black Street in East Jarrow. The façade of the house has been recreated as part of the Catherine Cookson display in the South Shields Museum and Art Gallery.

Picturesque Westhoe Village in the heart of South Shields is the backdrop for many of her books, including Katie Mulholland and Harrogate Street.

Visitors to the Christian heritage site Bede's World in Jarrow can see Jarrow Hall which was used as a setting for the televised version of one of her best loved novels, The Fifteen Streets.

In later life, the author returned with her husband Tom to live in the North East and Catherine Cookson fans include the couple's homes in Corbridge, Langley on Tyne and Jesmond (a suburb of Newcastle upon Tyne) in their literary pilgrimage.

Eight miles south-west of Newcastle upon Tyne is the Beamish Open Air Museum which depicts the lives of the type of characters Catherine Cookson wrote about.

A kiss is still a kiss

A fine romance

Mr Ken Smith of Swansea didn't care what the neighbours thought...

It was Easter 1986 when I made a life-changing journey from my home in Swansea to the Isle of Thanet in Kent. I was driving through the village of Birchington in my little blue mini when I saw a tall lady with the most beautiful smile.

She stepped out of her doorway and walked slowly towards the footpath. I turned the car round as quickly as I could and pulled up by the footpath. Then I jumped out of the car, ran round to where she stood, took her in my arms and kissed her.

Although she had never seen me before, she returned my kisses with equal fervour. I have to confess that our mutual attraction was not quite so spontaneous as it might appear. It had really begun some five months before this when I had returned home from work to find a letter waiting for me.

Recently divorced and living on my own, I had joined a Friendship Agency and the letter, which was from Elizabeth, was my first response. We clicked immediately and our daily letters were soon supplemented by daily telephone conversations.

Our meeting was arranged when I had to attend a conference in the area.

We have now been married for over 20 years and I still remember exactly what my Elizabeth was wearing – a navy-blue dress with little white spots, a Peter Pan collar, cap sleeves and white cuffs – when I first saw her. How many husbands can truly say that?

Happy Birthday

PIC: REX FEATURES

Do you know where and when your favourite movie stars were born? Simply match the star to their birth date and place. If you get stuck the answers are below.

1.	Audrey Hepburn	A.	Wellington, New Zealand, 1964
2.	Brigitte Bardot	B.	Ulverston, England, 1890
3.	Cary Grant	C.	Stockholm, Sweden, 1915
4.	Cliff Richard	D.	Rome, Italy, 1934
5.	Dan Ackroyd	E.	Pontrhydfen, Wales, 1925
6.	Doris Day	F.	Paris, France 1934
7.	Errol Flynn	G.	Ottawa, Ontario, Canada, 1952
8.	Frank Sinatra	H.	New York, USA, 1924
9.	Harrison Ford	I.	Lucknow, India, 1940
10.	Ingrid Bergman	J.	London, England, 1933
11.	James Stewart	K.	Ixelles, Brussles, Belgium, 1929
12.	Julie Christie	L.	Indiana, Pennsylvania, USA, 1908
13.	Lauren Bacall	M.	Hoboken, New Jersey, USA, 1915
14.	Michael Caine	N.	Hobart, Tasmania, Australia, 1909
15.	Omar Sharif	O.	Edinburgh, Scotland, UK, 1930
16.	Pierce Brosnan	P.	Drogheda, County Louth, Ireland, 1953
17.	Richard Burton	Q.	Cincinnati, Ohio, USA, 1924
18.	Russell Crowe	R.	Chukua, Assam, India, 1940
19.	Sean Connery	S.	Chicago, Illinois, USA, 1942
20.	Sofia Loren	T.	Bristol, England, 1904
21.	Stan Laurel	U.	Alexandria, Egypt, 1932

Answers: 1K, 2F, 3T, 4I, 5G, 6Q, 7N, 8M, 9S, 10C, 11L, 12R, 13H, 14J, 15U, 16P, 17E, 18A, 19O, 20D, 21B

A bad hair day

BY: KAREN CLARKE

Spring is in the air and Mo decides it's time for a change

I used to think that March should be consigned to the scrap heap of useless months. Nothing important in my life had ever happened in March – until I decided to walk out on Frank.

It wasn't really my idea. Left to myself, I'd have drifted on for another 30 years. It was other people, pointing out this and that about him. Things I hadn't noticed, to be honest. I hadn't looked at Frank properly for a long time.

My sister Flo said his greatest crime was being nondescript. "He's just there, lurking in the background," she complained.

Even the children had taken to criticising him.

"I love him to bits, but look at him, Mum," Sara said on one of her rare visit home. "He doesn't do anything since he gave up work. Unless you count pottering round the garden. He's no fun."

"How can you stick it?" Dan asked, the last time he popped in with his laundry. "He never wants to go out. It's not healthy."

Dan was studying psychology at uni. He added: "He's more interested in his birdwatching. I mean, who does that these days?'

I began to study Frank surreptitiously, and concluded they were right. An article I read in a magazine confirmed what I was thinking – a relationship based on exasperated fondness doesn't really cut the mustard these days.

So I decided to leave him. It was spring and the daffodils were bursting into bloom in a way that fuelled my restlessness.

"You should go while you're young enough to start over," my friend Dee advised. She had left her Geoffrey when their youngest emigrated to Australia. She'd sold their house, lost a stone in weight and gone on a cruise before moving in with a builder from Croydon.

"You and Frank never had that magic spark"

She said: "You and Frank never had that magic spark, but it's not too late, Mo. Look at me and Kevin."

I packed a suitcase, fed the cat and got a bus into town. I decided I'd phone Frank when I got to wherever I was going.

I sat in the park for a good half hour. There was a band playing near the river. A few people were dancing in a carefree way and I longed to join them, but years of being inhibited held me back.

Reluctantly, I moved on and hovered outside the travel agent on Bridge Street, feeling a little silly. I had a sneaking suspicion that being impulsive didn't suit me.

Staring at my reflection in the window I saw a bubble perm, a lined face and an overweight body in a sensible belted mac. Why was I wearing a mac? It wasn't even cold. On an impulse, I shrugged it off and stuffed it in a rubbish bin.

At that moment, I saw my next-door neighbour heading towards me and quickly dived through the nearest door. I couldn't cope with questions.

Willing her to walk past, I stared hard at the spotless counter in front of me.

"Good morning, Madam, my name is Lucy. What time's your appointment?"

A pretty girl with a pierced eyebrow tilted her head, enquiringly.

"Doesn't that hurt?" I asked, without thinking.

"This?" She twiddled the tiny stud, smiling at me. "Not really. I fancied a bit of a change. Do you like it?"

"It's lovely," I said, and it was. Smooth and shiny against her skin.

Lucy looked pleased. "Now, what time did you say your appointment was?" She flicked through a diary, and I realised

ILLUSTRATION: KATE DAVIES

I had time to think about Frank while Lucy worked her magic. Maybe I'd become a habit for him, too

something with this," Lucy said. "The perm has almost grown out. I could put some fresh colour in, warm it up a bit. Maybe get Julie to tidy your eyebrows."

I started to feel something that might have been excitement.

"A new image," I said, and in the mirror a woman with flushed cheeks and bright eyes smiled back at me.

"Your husband won't recognise you," she laughed, catching my mood.

I had time to think about Frank while Lucy worked her magic. Maybe I'd become a habit for him, too. I thought of him in his beloved garden, carefully nurturing my favourite plants year in, year out. Careful. That was the word, not nondescript.

Above the noise of the hairdryer, Lucy was asking: "Where is it you're going, then?"

"Birdwatching," I said, without missing a beat. "I'm going birdwatching with my husband."

I was in a hairdresser's. The expensive one with tinted windows and posters of bored-looking models.

"Oh, I – er – was just passing," I said, going hot with embarrassment. They wouldn't be used to old fogies like me in here.

"That's all right," Lucy said, kindly. "We're not very busy on Mondays. I can do you now, if you like. What was it you wanted?"

That stumped me. I hadn't set foot inside a hairdressing salon for 15 years. I usually coloured my hair at home, and trimmed bits off with the kitchen scissors.

"Come and sit down and we'll have a look at you," Lucy offered, coming out from behind the counter. She loomed over me in her spikey heels, but her touch was gentle. "Bring your suitcase through. Going away are you? Is that why you fancy a new hairdo?"

"Sort of," I said, still blushing.

Obediently, I followed her across the gleaming wood floor and let her settle me into a soft, leather chair. When she ran her fingers through my tangled curls it was so relaxing I forgot to feel mortified..

"We could really do

April 2009

Wednesday
1
All Fools' Day

Thursday
2

Friday
3

Saturday
4

Sunday
5
Palm Sunday

Monday
6

Tuesday
7

Wednesday
8

Thursday
9
Maundy Thursday

Friday
10
Good Friday

Saturday
11

Sunday
12
Easter Sunday

Monday
13
Easter Monday

Tuesday
14

Wednesday
15

Thursday
16

Friday
17

Saturday
18

Sunday
19

Monday
20

Tuesday
21
HM Queen Elizabeth's II's birthday

Wednesday
22

Thursday	Monday
23 St George's Day	**27**
Friday	Tuesday
24	**28**
Saturday	Wednesday
25	**29**
Sunday	Thursday
26 Flora London Marathon	**30**

Behind the Scenes

Becket, 1964

Fresh from the machinations of the Roman Empire in the film Cleopatra (1963), Richard Burton swaps Mark Antony's toga for an archbishop's robes the following year, as saintly Thomas Becket in the movie, Becket.

As a monk glides by the background, Elizabeth Taylor, who's visiting him on set, gives him what can only be described as a Cleopatra-like look of devotion, as Richard lounges in his costume. The wardrobe master would probably have something to say about the creases.

But his costume was probably the last thing on his mind. Taylor and Burton worked together for the first time on Cleopatra, marrying in March 1964, four days after the release of Becket – which accounts for that look of love.

But just as Becket, 'the turbulent priest' was at odds with King Henry II, the Burtons' marriage was similarly tempestuous, they having married twice – and divorced…

Schooldays remembered

Eight-year-old Audrey outside the school gates in 1949

I went to Grange Park Infants and Juniors School Sunderland until 1956, when I passed my eleven plus and to Monkwearmouth Grammar School.

I was a teacher's pet at junior school – the teachers called me Auntie Cowie. That's because my eldest sister was already married and had her first baby when I was eight years old (and my maiden name was Cowie).

I was sent to other classes doing messages – I don't know how I ever learned anything. I was also a monitor for classroom attendance books, delivering and collecting them.

My mother allowed me to wear my Sunday best clothes on a Monday, and the teachers used to remark how pretty I looked.

The other children used to pick on me, but I soon got my own back – I was one of the best fighters in school. I could bite, nip, scratch and pull hair! Charming, wasn't I?

Audrey Faul, Hartlepool

My Grandparents

One day when I visited my Grandfather at his home in Oxhill (I was three) I was fascinated by a small pedal harmonium which was in the living room. Granddad was a lay preacher on the Wesleyan circuit and loved his music very much.

I was obsessed by all things musical from an early age (playing on the table leaf to accompany my singing) so naturally I asked Granddad if I could try the harmonium, and he said I could. But better still, if I could go off and remember a hymn, and could come back and play it through for him, then I could have the harmonium to keep.

I was thrilled and duly went home to remember a hymn, and when I next went to Granddad's, I played the hymn with both hands. Granddad was astounded, he didn't really think I'd be able to play like that, and so the organ was mine.

We managed to get it home on a carrier's van, and I played the instrument morning, noon and night.

From the organ I progressed to an ancient piano, and so began my love affair with playing organ

and piano – and it all began with Granddad's little harmonium. Sadly, he died in 1948, the year after he gave me his precious gift. He would be so pleased to know that I have had such pleasure from it.

Ethel Davies, Stratford-upon-Avon, Warks

Left: Ethel's Grandparents, Sam and Annie Coleman, with Ethel's mum, Edith May. Photo taken 1903. Right: Ethel, aged three

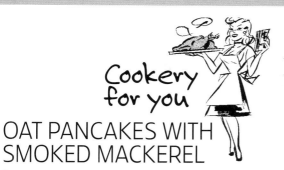

Cookery for you

OAT PANCAKES WITH SMOKED MACKEREL

Serves 4

- ◆ 110 g (4 oz) pinhead oatmeal, toasted
- ◆ 4 tablespoons chopped parsley, plus extra to garnish
- ◆ 4 medium eggs, beaten
- ◆ 100 ml (3¹/₂ fl oz) crème fraîche
- ◆ 1 tablespoon horseradish sauce
- ◆ 300 g (11 oz) smoked mackerel fillets
- ◆ 1 tablespoon olive or sunflower oil

1 Mix together the oatmeal, parsley and eggs and season. Leave to stand for 10 minutes.
2 Mix the crème fraîche with the horseradish sauce.
3 Flake the fish into large pieces, discarding the skin.
4 Heat the oil in a large, heavy-based frying pan. Place 4 ladlesfull of the oatmeal mixture into the pan, spacing them slightly apart. Cook gently and try to keep the cakes compact. When the bottom is golden brown, turn the cakes over and cook for a further 15 seconds.
Place on 4 serving plates and pile the fish on top. Add a spoonful of the crème fraiche mixture to each and scatter with extra parsley.

THAT'S INTERESTING...

Television's first – and most famous – April Fools' hoaxes was the spoof documentary on April 1, 1957 about spaghetti crops, narrated by Richard Dimbleby.

Colourful climbers
Clematis macropetala

This clematis cultivar is covered with plummy pink double flowers during April. These are followed by attractive whiskery seed-heads in autumn. Like all early-flowering clematis, it requires little pruning other than the removal of any dead or damaged growth after flowering. It enjoys full sun or partial shade, copes with most types of soil and easily reaches 3m in height. Plants widely available.

TOP TIP

Buy a pack of facial wipes and keep them in your handbag and use to spot clean any unforeseen stains – especially useful when wearing white jeans!

Colleen Watson, Herne Bay, Kent

Healthier for longer!

Eat an apple a day – it could keep dementia away. Apples and other fruits such as bananas and oranges contain a type of anti-oxidant which could help to prevent toxic free radicals from damaging your brain cells and help to reduce your risk of problems such as Alzheimer's.

April 6 - 12

Cookery for you

HOT CHOCOLATE FONDANT PUDDINGS

Serves 6

- ◆ 50 g (2 oz) butter
- ◆ 75 g (3 oz) caster sugar
- ◆ 170 g (6 oz) Carnation condensed milk
- ◆ 4 large eggs, beaten with a pinch of salt
- ◆ 1 teaspoon vanilla extract
- ◆ 1 tablespoon strong coffee powder, dissolved in 1 tablespoon boiling water
- ◆ 350 g (12 oz) dark chocolate, melted
- ◆ 75 g (3 oz) plain flour
- ◆ Icing sugar, to dust

1 Preheat the oven to 200°C/400°F/Gas Mark 6. Place a large baking sheet in the oven.
2 Grease and base line six 150 ml (¼ pt) Dariole moulds or pudding basins.
3 Beat together the butter and sugar until pale and creamy. Gradually whisk in the condensed milk.
4 Gently whisk in the eggs a little at a time, followed by the vanilla and coffee. Add the chocolate, mix thoroughly, then add the flour and whisk until smooth.
5 Divide the mixture between the moulds. Place them onto the hot baking sheet and bake for 10 minutes.
6 Immediately run a knife around the mould to loosen, and dust with icing sugar. Serve with vanilla ice cream.

Recipe courtesy Nestlé Carnation, www.carnation.co.uk

My Grandparents

I am now 78, but I still remember my Grandmother telling me, with a twinkle in her eye, that when she was young, (in the 1890s) the news spread like wildfire, 'that Louie hasn't got her bustle on!'

Jill Hayward, London SW4

Left: Louisa Letitia Fowler

TOP TIP

To descale a washing machine, put a cup of vinegar in the detergent dispenser and run the machine empty on a hot cycle.

Healthier for longer!

Measure your waist – it should be below 32 inches if you're a woman and 37 inches if you're a man. Anything higher than this and you're at an increased risk of health problems such as heart disease and diabetes.

THAT'S INTERESTING...

Easter is always the first Sunday after the first full moon after the Spring Equinox (which is March 20 or 21). This dating of Easter is based on the lunar calendar that Hebrew people used to identify Passover, which is why it moves around on our Roman calendar.

Schooldays remembered

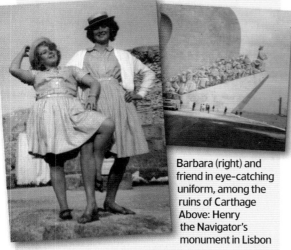

Barbara (right) and friend in eye-catching uniform, among the ruins of Carthage
Above: Henry the Navigator's monument in Lisbon

I went on an educational Mediterranean cruise with my school in April 1964, on board the Dunera. We boarded at Southampton and sailed to Tangier, Tunis, Malaga and Lisbon at a cost of £45. I still have the log book and itinery, though I only filled it in for the first two days.

I was in Hawkins dormitory and we slept in bunks which were help up with chains, and which were easy to dismantle, so it wasn't unusual to find your bed was missing!

Our first port of call was Tangier where I bartered for a set of bongo drums made from rather smelly camel skin. We set sail for Tunis in rather choppy waters – several friends kept disappearing to hang over the side of the ship.

After the heat of Tunis, our next stop was Malaga, where we boarded a rickety old bus and set off on a hairy drive to Granada to visit the Alhambra. On the way back down, we saw another bus that had gone over the edge – we spent the rest of the journey with our eyes shut.

Lastly we sailed to Lisbon, and I remember being very impressed by Prince Henry the Navigator's monument.

Dressed in our summer dresses and straw boaters, we attracted attention wherever we went and must have looked like beings from another planet to the locals!

Ruth Ritchie, York

Meeting the stars

Having been a huge fan of Sir Terry Wogan for many years, and an avid listener of his Radio 2 programme, imagine my delight to hear he was book signing locally, in Windsor. I was nearly first in the queue!

What a lovely man he is; on seeing all his fans, he said: "Goodness me, is someone famous coming here today?"

Shirley McCulley, Camberely, Surrey

Shirley with Sir Terry

Colourful climbers
Glory bower

An uncommon choice, Clerodendrum thomsoniae, the bleeding heart or glory bower hails from Western Central Africa. Although tender, the warmth of a heated conservatory may prompt it to start flowering as early as April, when it produces attractive red and white flowers. These are followed by inedible black and orange-red berries. Seeds are available from Jungle Seeds at www.jungleseeds.co.uk

Cookery for you

KALE BUBBLE & SQUEAK WITH CHORIZO

Serves 4

- ◆ 800 g (1 lb 10 oz) floury potatoes, diced
- ◆ 200 g (7 oz) kale, shredded
- ◆ 225 g (8 oz) chorizo sausage, diced
- ◆ 2 medium leeks, sliced
- ◆ 1 tablespoon sunflower oil

1. Boil the potatoes and kale for 10-12 minutes, or until tender, and drain.
2. Meanwhile, fry the chorizo and leeks for 7-8 minutes.
3. Add the potatoes and Kale and fry for 1-2 minutes.
   Crush lightly with a potato masher and season to taste.

Tip: For a vegetarian option, replace the chorizo with a 400g (13 oz) tin of kidney beans.

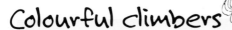

Colourful climbers

Black–Eyed Susan

Thunbergia grandiflora is a popular garden plant but if you want colour early in the year, try growing it in a conservatory. As a half-hardy annual, it flowers in summer when grown outside, but from March onwards when protected by glass. Several different varieties are available, all of which will twine attractively up a small archway. It enjoys a sunny position and moist, well-drained compost. Seeds widely available.

Recipe courtesy www.discoverkale.co.uk

THAT'S INTERESTING...

The phrase, 'You could have knocked me down with a feather' was probably introduced by Charles Dickens. In David Copperfield, Dr Chillip says, 'You might have knocked me down on the flat of my back, sir, with the feather of a pen'.

And 'what the dickens' was in use long before Charles Dickens made the surname famous. The word 'Dickens', used as a substitute for one that might be offensive – was a diminutive form of Richard, to replace 'Old Nick' or the 'devil'.

Healthier for longer!

Try hawthorn – taking a hawthorn supplement could help to lower your cholesterol and boost your anti-oxidant levels to keep your heart healthy according to US scientists. Try Viridian Hawthorn Berry Capsules from health stores. But see your GP first for advice.

My Grandparents

My Nan Flora – Florrie to most – but Nan to my brother and I, was widowed at 38 and left with two boys – my Dad, aged 16 and his elder brother. Granddad was lost at sea in January 1940.

Nan ran a general grocery shop selling all sorts, including wool and makeup. I spent as much time as I could with Nan, helping out in the shop. One of my earliest memories was standing at the shop door collecting ration books as customers came in.

I also used to love sitting in cardboard boxes just inside the shop door, and one day the vegetable delivery man came in, in a hurry, and tipped a load of cauliflowers over my head. Another memory was sitting under the counter weighing up sugar and putting it into blue bags.

On her half day off we'd sometimes take the bus into Eccles for afternoon tea, and on other occasions we'd go to the theatre. I remember going to a Christmas play on Boxing Day to see A Christmas Carol, a very young Michael Caine playing Bob Cratchit

As she got older she went to live with her elder son in Essex and helped him in their pub. When I got married, she let my husband and I live in her bungalow, and we were not allowed to pay a penny in rent, which enabled us to save for our first house.

Barbara Utton, Lowestoft, Suffolk

Below: Nan Flora with two-year-old Barbara

Schooldays remembered

About 1946, Mum, Dad, my brother and I lived with my grandparents in Dagenham, and their house backed onto the school I went to.

One day at Infants school, we were in the school hall and the teacher was choosing children for the choir. After hearing my singing voice (I had a low gruff voice then – and I still do!) I was told I couldn't join.

Unperturbed, I left the hall and walked round the corner home! Popa (granddad) was home and asked me why I was home so early, so I explained they didn't want me in the choir, so I came home.

After some TLC, he took me back to school. It was an incident that Popa remembered and told me, and which still made him laugh many years later! And I still can't sing…

May Oldrey, Romford, Essex

May in 1946

May's 'Popa

Cookery for you

BLACKCURRANT SORBET

Serves 4

- ◆ 200 g (7 oz) blackcurrants
- ◆ Juice of medium orange
- ◆ 225 g (8 oz) caster sugar
- ◆ 275 ml (¹/₂ pint) water

1 Boil the water and dissolve the sugar in it. Turn to a low heat for two minutes, then remove and leave to cool.
2 Use a blender or food processor to purée the blackcurrants. Sieve the purée to remove pips to leave a smooth mixture.
3 Combine the purée with the orange juice, and then with the sugar solution and mix well.
4 Place in a lidded freezer-proof container in the freezer for 2-3 hours.
5 Remove from freezer and stir again. Return to the freezer until set. Serve in scoops.

Recipe courtesy The Blackcurrant Foundation

My Grandparents

Granny Sample with Ann (in the white bonnet) and her brothers and sister

It was 1940/41 and there were air raids over Sunderland. I was four or five years old, and still remember being carried out to the air raid shelter and seeing the search lights shining over the dark starry sky.

One night we didn't get out in time; the rest of the family was in the cupboard under the stairs, and Granny Sample and I were under the kitchen table.

We had a little Yorkshire Terrier called Gyp, and he kept going from the family to us under the table.

Granny's tummy kept rumbling and Gyp stood there wondering where the noise was coming from.

Ann Harriman, Harrogate, N Yorks

Healthier for longer!

Eat your greens – it could protect your eyesight. Dark green leafy vegetables such as kale, spinach, watercress, broccoli and cabbage are crammed with the antioxidants lutein and zeaxanthin which researchers have found could help to prevent cataracts.

▌ THAT'S INTERESTING...

Ketchup started out as a general term for sauce, typically made of mushrooms or fish brine with herbs and spices. Some early main ingredients included blueberry, anchovy, oyster, lobster, kidney beans and walnuts.

Schooldays remembered

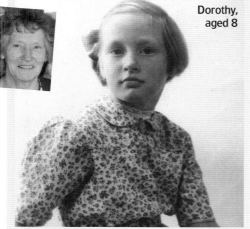

Dorothy, aged 8

My first school was in a small village, and there were only about 15 pupils at any time, aged from four upwards.

The school consisted of one main room, with a small room divided off. This contained the coke fed stove; there was always a clothes maiden to one side, on which gloves, socks and coats were hung out to dry. During the really cold weather the partition was pulled back for extra warmth.

The toilets at my little school were, of course, outside, and swallows used to nest in the roof of the boys' toilets, while ours were regularly occupied by a toad which, as we were country children, didn't bother us at all.

The children helped to look after the garden, and sometimes we were allowed to take some produce home. I can still remember getting into trouble when I presented the teacher with a bunch of all the flowers I had carefully picked from the strawberry patch.

Dorothy Bloor, Leek, Staffs

TOP TIP

Cut carnations and pinks last a long time if you put them in lemonade, but change it every few days, just as you would water.

Colourful climbers
C montana 'Elisabeth'

Clematis are one of the most popular climbers and the easiest to grow is C montana. It thrives in sun or partial shadeand copes with all but the wettest soils. It grows vigorously and is excellent when used to cover an unsightly shed, wall or fence, producing masses of flowers between late spring and early summer. Little pruning is required, but they can be cut hard back, almost to ground level if they get woody. Height 8m. AGM. Plants widely available.

Meeting the stars

We were on holiday in Nerja on the Costa del Dol in 2005 and imagine my delight to find some of the Emmerdale cast staying in our hotel as they were filming on location further up town. Each day they would come down to breakfast, then go off in mini-buses for the day's filming.

One morning, we asked Steve Halliwell, who plays Zak Dingle if we could take a photograph, and he was most obliging.

Elaine Thomas, Mansfield, Notts

'Zak' and Elaine

Shropshire: Ellis Peters Country

Magical marches

Better known to the world by her pen name of Ellis Peters, Edith Pargeter was born at Horsehay in Shropshire in 1913 and, apart from serving with Women's Royal Navy Service during the Second World War, lived there until she died in 1995.

After attending Coalbrookdale High School for Girls, she worked as a chemist's assistant in Dawley and used some of the knowledge she gained in later crime novels. The most famous of these are the ones featuring Brother Cadfael, a Benedictine monk who is a skilled herbalist.

The medieval crime solver first appeared in A Morbid Taste for Bones published in 1977 and a further 18 Brother Cadfael books followed, many set in the dramatic landscape of the Welsh Marches. A number of different car trails and walks take in locations such as the ruins of Buildwas Abbey (where the hermit Cuthred lodged in The Hermit of Eyton Forest) and the tiny village of Llansilin (mentioned in Monk's Hood and Dead Man's Ransom).

No visit to Shropshire would be complete without exploring the county town of Shrewsbury with its timber-framed buildings and steep narrow streets. Shrewsbury Abbey has a memorial to Ellis Peters.

Other attractions include one of the best preserved 13th century fortified manor houses in the country – Stokesay Castle near the Welsh border.

The joker in the pack

Ah! Happy days

Enid Robson of Newcastle–upon–Tyne grew up when coal was king

My parents spent most of their lives in the small mining village of New Herrington. There were two pits: the Dorothea, known locally as the Dolly and the New Pit which was where my father worked from leaving school at the age of 14.

My mother was small and fair-haired and seemed always to be in the kitchen making meals at different times of the day to coincide with Dad's shifts. Food was still on ration after the Second World War and meat was expensive but Dad grew lots of vegetables.

Dad was a little taller than Mum and had black curly hair. He loved his garden and had a great sense of humour. Once he took

his wheelbarrow up to the nearby farm to get some manure. It smelt awful and I asked him what he was going to do with it. He said: "Go and tell your Mam to make some custard for tea and we'll

have some of this with it."

I was horrified but when I told Mam, she just laughed – Dad was only pulling my leg.

Many miners were superstitious. One superstition was that before going to work a miner should always say 'good morning' to his wife and must not leave until she had answered him.

One April Fool's day, when my father was on an early shift, he woke Mam, saying: "I have slept in. Can you get up and help me get ready for work."

Mam got up and made his bait and a cup of tea, then Dad came downstairs and said: "April Fool!" It was 2.45 am. I don't know what Mam said to him but we laughed about it years afterwards.

Famous One Liners

Can you match these memorable movie one liners to the films they came from? If you get stuck the answers are below

PIC: REX FEATURES

1.	"Stupid is as stupid does."	A.	Willy Wonka and the Chocolate Factory
2.	"That'll be the day."	B.	The Wizard of Oz
3.	"We're gonna need a bigger boat!"	C.	The Searchers
4.	"Fasten your seatbelts, it's going to be a bumpy night!"	D.	The Life of Brian
5.	"I coulda been a contender."	E.	Taxi Driver
6.	"You talkin' to me?"	F.	Some Like it Hot
7.	"You can't handle the truth!"	G.	On the Waterfront
8.	"We're alike, me and cat. A couple of poor nameless slobs."	H.	My Fair Lady
9.	"Do I feel lucky? Well, do ya, punk?"	I.	Jaws
10.	"I'm a good girl, I am!"	J.	Gone With The Wind
11.	"I always get the fuzzy end of the lollipop."	K.	Forrest Gump
12.	"They all turn into blueberries in the end!"	L.	Dirty Harry
13.	"He's not the Messiah, he's a very naughty boy!"	M.	Breakfast at Tiffany's
14.	"There's no place like home."	N.	All About Eve
15.	"Frankly, my dear, I don't give a damn!"	O.	A Few Good Men

Answers: 1K, 2C, 3I, 4N, 5G, 6E, 7O, 8M, 9L, 10H, 11F, 12A, 13D, 14B, 15J

Cushioning the

BY: PENNY PECORELLI

Sometimes a kindly meant gift can be taken the wrong way...

Jenny unwrapped her present. "I hope you'll like it," her friend Jane said.

"Oh, it's a cushion – how lovely!" exclaimed Jenny. Then she saw the message embroidered on it: 'It's not that I'm bossy – I'm just a born leader'.

"Oh," she murmured. "Oh, thanks, it's… it's terrific." She leaned forward to kiss Jane's cheek.

"I hope it's all right?"

Jenny could see Jane was worried. "I mean – I thought you'd find it amusing."

"Yes, yes, it's great. Very funny." Jenny tried to sound bright and breezy.

"You're not offended?"

"No, of course not. You're right – it's very… um… amusing. Thank you so much."

"Oh, you are offended! I thought you'd see the funny side…" Jane's voice tailed off.

"Jane, it's a great cushion. Thank you for remembering my birthday," said Jenny firmly.

"You're my special friend," Jane reassured her. "You know that, don't you?"

"Thanks," said Jenny, more warmly, "I do."

"Doug?" said Jenny to her husband later that evening while they were celebrating her birthday with a special dinner.

"Mmm?" he said, through a mouthful of vegetables.

"Am I very bossy?"

There was a long pause. Maybe, thought Jenny hopefully, it was because he was finishing his mouthful of food. He surely didn't need time to consider the answer?

She knew she was decisive by nature, but that wasn't the same thing as being bossy, was it? Was it?

"Of course not," said Doug eventually, after he'd swallowed.

"You're sure?"

"Sure" he said, smiling. "You're decisive, that's all. It's a good thing. I hate ditherers."

"You're decisive, that's all. It's a good thing. I hate ditherers"

But Jenny thought that there was something in his expression that told her otherwise.

"Thanks," she said, unsurely.

"Don't worry about it – it's your birthday," he said.

But she did worry about it. The thought niggled away at her. How awful if that was how people saw her – ordering them about, riding roughshod over their opinions. Was she really like that?

Usually a good sleeper, Jenny found herself waking in the early hours, casting her mind back to times when she might have been bossy.

She had been unanimously elected Chair of the Parish Council. Did that mean she was seen as a capable person – or a bossy one?

She thought about her three sons. She had brought them up, she hoped, to be thoughtful of others. She had a horror of badly behaved children and had been firm with her own – as well as with the odd young scamp she caught running riot on the village green. She gave them a good ticking off, but that was her duty as a citizen, wasn't it?

And Doug? Did she boss Doug about? Surely not. When she suggested he changed his tie to one that went better with his suit, that wasn't being bossy, was it?

Then she thought of the time he'd jokingly introduced her to one of his friends. "Jenny, this is Pete," he had said. "Pete, meet the Boss."

She had joined in the laughter, taking it as a joke in the same category as calling your wife Her Indoors. But, perhaps, he really did see her as his boss?

"Jamie," she asked her youngest son, home for half-term. "Would you say I was bossy?"

blow

He grinned: "No more than most mothers. I mean you had three lively boys to keep in order, didn't you?"

"So, am I?"

"Well, when you want to be, I suppose. Hey, Mum, what's brought this on? I didn't mean bossy in a bad way – just firm. Why are you so upset?"

She showed him the cushion.

Jamie roared with laughter and said: "Don't worry. You're a great mum and if you put us in our place, I'm sure we deserved it. When's lunch? I'm starving."

At the next Parish Council meeting Jenny was unusually subdued. She allowed some interruptions from Mrs Harris, the village busybody, to go on far too long.

"Are you all right?" asked her friend Sally after the meeting. "You're very quiet. Are you feeling ill?"

"I'm fine," said Jenny, "I just felt it would be nice to let other people have a say."

"Well, you usually keep better control and don't let Mrs Harris ramble on for hours."

"Oh dear, I suppose she did. Sorry."

As they left the village hall they noticed smoke coming from the adjoining shed. Someone shouted, 'Fire!' and panic broke out.

Jenny hesitated only for a moment. Making sure everyone was outside, she did a quick head count.

"Sally," she said. "Call the fire brigade on your mobile." Turning to another committee member, she instructed: "Fred, there's a fire extinguisher inside the entrance. Fetch that, will you?"

"Now, Mrs Harris," said Jenny, "Why don't you pop over to your house and make everyone a nice cup of tea."

When Mrs Harris returned with a tray of mugs, the firemen had dealt with the blaze.

"I'll bet it was those lads up the road smoking in there," said Fred.

Sally turned to Jenny: "I really do admire your ability to take control."

"You mean be bossy," replied Jenny wryly.

"Bossy? No!" exclaimed Sally. "Whoever said you are bossy? You're just a born leader."

May 2009

Friday
1

Saturday
2

Sunday
3

Monday
4

Early May Bank Holiday

Tuesday
5

Wednesday
6

Thursday
7

Friday
8

Saturday
9

Sunday
10

Monday
11

Tuesday
12

Wednesday
13

Thursday
14

Friday
15

Saturday
16

Sunday
17

Monday
18

Tuesday
19

Wednesday
20

Thursday
21

Ascension Day

Friday
22

Saturday 23	**Thursday** 28
Sunday 24	**Friday** 29
Monday 25	**Saturday** 30
Spring Bank Holiday	
Tuesday 26	**Sunday** 31
	Pentecost (Whitsun)
Wednesday 27	

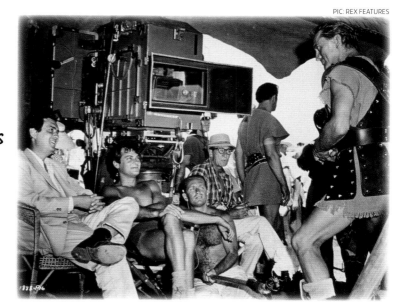

Behind the Scenes

Spartacus, 1960

A cleft chin, eyes of steel and showing a comely leg, that's Kirk Douglas as he pauses to talk to Tony Curtis and other members of the cast and production crew of the film Spartacus, in 1960.

The virile Kirk was just the right man to play the rebellious slave Spartacus, who leads a violent revolt against the decadent Roman empire. He had a great cast of notables alongside him, including Laurence Olivier, Jean Simmons, Peter Ustinov and Herbert Lom (playing a Scilian pirate – a far cry from the twitchy-eyed Inspector Dreyfuss in The Pink Panther!).

Looking relaxed and tanned sitting near the camera is the equally handsome Tony Curtis. Kirk and Tony had starred together a couple of years before in another bloodthirsty epic, The Vikings – playing half brothers. Funny, they don't look anything like each other…

My Grandparents

My Grandparents, John and Eliza McCulloch, had ten children, six boys and four girls, my mother being fourth from youngest.

My life revolved around my own home and my Grandparents' home. We went to Grandma's for tea every Monday, Wednesday and Saturday. One Aunt and Uncle never left home, and we used to sit round the table after tea and play dominoes and snap, and there was always lots of conversation.

My Aunt and Grandma were good seamstresses and made many of my dresses. I remember standing on the large kitchen table to have my hems adjusted. When I was four, I had the measles and cried to go and 'be poorly on Grandma's couch'.

Sadly, Grandpa died when I was seven, but Grandma lived until she was 92 years old. The three times a week visits continued throughout my adult life and only stopped when I married and moved 20 miles away. I was delighted that Grandma was able to visit us, just once, in our first home.

E Irene Spencer, Carlisle, Cumbria
Eliza and John, circa 1930, taken on
their Golden Wedding anniversary

Healthier for longer!

Add more olive oil to your cooking – it contains polyphenols, natural antioxidants which help to slow down the rate at which your body's cells age according to Spanish scientists. Drizzle the extra virgin version over salads to get all the benefits.

Colourful climbers
Akebia quinata

The chocolate vine is a beautiful semi-evergreen climber with attractive dark green leaves that are blue-green beneath, then tinged purple in winter. Producing racemes of spicy, chocolate-scented flowers followed by large pink fruit, it grows quickly, making it ideal for covering a plain fence. Give it full sun and free-draining soil and it may reach 10m in height. Plants widely available.

THAT'S INTERESTING...

It's May at last, when the garden beckons ...

◆ Apparently, 55% of the population spend two or more hours a week gardening.

'Gardening adds years to your life and life to your years' **Anon**

A swarm of bees in May
Is worth a load of hay
A swarm of bees in June
Is worth a silver spoon
A swarm of bees in July
Is not worth a fly.
Anon

◆ Do not drive a bee out of the house because you drive out your good luck

Schooldays remembered

I have various memories: The Maypole in the hall, and two boys were chosen to sit, one either side, to hold it, while others played the triangle or the tambourine. The rest of the class would dance, holding the colourful braids and getting them in a terrible tangle. The teacher would bounce up from the piano and shout at us until we trembled.

I loved to look in the museum cabinet, as I was very proud of a giant moth which I'd caught in an air raid shelter. I trapped it in a jam jar and took it to school. The next time I saw it, it was pinned on a display board in the cabinet, with its Latin name, and my name under it.

One little girl's father was an air steward, so would bring back some beautiful dolls for her, and she brought them to show us, but we weren't allowed to touch.

When the 'nit nurse' came, we had to line up while she turned everyone's hair up to the front and the back. Some poor little souls were tersely told to stand to one side, and we all knew they'd got nits, and were cruelly teased by some of the boys at playtime.

**Eileen Newman,
Bolsover, Derbys**

OATMEAL AND DILL CRUSTED SALMON

Serves: 4

Cookery for you

◆ 4 salmon fillets
◆ 1 tablespoon olive oil
◆ 3-4 tablespoons oatmeal
◆ 1 tablespoon fresh dill, chopped
◆ 1 lemon, finely grated zest and juice
◆ Dill sprigs to garnish

1 Lightly brush the top of each salmon fillet with olive oil. Preheat grill to a medium heat.
2 Line a grill pan with foil and place the fish, flesh side up, on the grill rack.
3 Mix the oatmeal with the dill, lemon zest and seasoning. Sprinkle the mixture evenly over the salmon fillets. Pat down lightly to give a good coating and grill for 8-10 minutes, without turning.
4 Serve garnished with fresh dill.

Recipe courtesy www.allaboutoats.com

Cookery for you

ETON MESS

Serves 4

- ◆ 8 meringue nests
- ◆ 750 ml (1¼ pint) double cream
- ◆ 110 g (4 oz) caster sugar
- ◆ 1 teaspoon vanilla essence
- ◆ 150 g (5 oz) strawberries, halved
- ◆ 150 g (5 oz) blackberries
- ◆ 150 g (5 oz) raspberries
- ◆ 1 tablespoon Grand Marnier (optional)
- ◆ Grated zest of 1 orange

1 Break the meringue nests into large pieces.
2 Whip the cream with the sugar and vanilla essence until stiff. Fold in the broken pieces of meringue, strawberries, blackberries and raspberries, Grand Marnier and orange zest.
3 Spoon mixture into individual bowls and garnish with additional berries if desired. Serve immediately.

Recipe courtesy British Asparagus Growers' Association, www.british-asparagus.co.uk and Rachel Green

My Grandparents

My paternal grandparents, Amelia and Tom Minney, were very special to me, as I was their only grandchild and I went to live with them when my mother died.

Granddad would tell me stories of his time as a cornet player in a brass band – he also had a wonderful sense of humour which at times caused a stern look from Grandma.

We'd go to the park where there was a museum, and I would beg her to take me to see a model of a lady making lace, and Grandma would tell me how she'd made lace when she was young.

We'd then go outside and I would off to the people playing bowls, as this would fascinate me. She said I might play it one day, and I said, 'not until I'm old', and she laughed. As bowls is now a great hobby of mine, and I don't consider myself old, I wonder what she would say!

Amelia and Tom with Sue and Patsy the dog in 1946

As my Granddad and Dad died within four years of each other, my Grandma and I became very close. She had great foresight and was right in so many things. She used to say that I would, 'remember the old girl when she was long gone'. I don't think there's a day goes by without me thinking about her.

Sue Stevenson, Buckland St Mary, Somerset

Healthier for longer!

Stock up on strawberries – they could help to reduce levels of a c-reactive protein in your body which could lead to inflammation of your blood vessels and increase your risk of having a stroke or heart attack, say Harvard Scientists. Just go easy on the cream (just this once, then, with the Eton Mess!)

■ THAT'S INTERESTING...

There are many sayings about brooms including, 'Brooms bought in May sweep families away.'

Colourful climbers
Actinidia kolomikta

Slightly tender, this unusual climber thrives in a sunny position and light, well-drained soils. Vigorous and twining, it's grown for its heart-shaped leaves which, when mature, are variegated pink and cream at the tips. A dramatic species for covering a large wall, it looks most spectacular against a background of old brick. It flowers during the summer but its blooms are insignificant. Height 5m. Plants widely available.

Meeting the stars

When I left school in 1960, I was a shy and gauche girl, working as a chambermaid in a hotel in Bagshot, Surrey. One morning, I served tea to a portly gentleman in his room who was, I later discovered, none other than Alfred Hitchcock.

But my greatest claim to meeting the stars was in the 1990s. I was appearing in an amateur production of Lettice and Lovage by Peter Shaffer, at the Bracknell Arts Centre which was directed by Joyce Harper.

On the opening night, all went well and Joyce popped her head round the dressing room door and said there was someone she wanted us to meet. "This is my brother Ken," she announced, as Ken Branagh stepped forward to greet us.

He shook hands and praised our acting. His visit was brief as he was off to begin filming.
Sylvia Washington, Wellington, Somerset

PIC: REX FEATURES

Schooldays remembered

My schooldays were mostly in the 1940s. I was always included in the Mayday celebrations, either as a flower girl (a daffodil), in the dancing or the choir, and finally in the Queen's procession. Singing was my forte and I really enjoyed it – still do.
Patricia Pegg, Sheffield, S Yorks

Mayday celebrations at Patricia's school

Schooldays remembered

I went to Kendal High School, Westmoreland in the 1940s. Our uniform was Kendal Green – a tunic, blazer, beret, white blouse with green tie, and thick brown lisle stockings.

Our lunches were generally good – my favourite was mince, mashed potatoes and peas, followed by creamy rice pudding, or jam squares and custard. I had free school meals, so always ate plenty – after once eating seven jam squares, the teacher asked me if I always ate like that at home! I also had two free bottles of milk a day. With our morning milk, we would queue up to get a warm 1d currant bun with a sticky sugary top – mmm!

In the school grounds was a beautiful Siberian Crab Apple tree, always laden with fruit each year, which we would chew on at break time while laying under it looking for four-leafed clovers.

Part of the grounds was made into allotments for anyone who wanted to 'grow their own'. My sister and I had one, and we grew lots of vegetables. We were so keen that we always got an A or A* for our efforts.

The only lesson I didn't like was history, so I was allowed to drop it after getting only 7% in my last exam. Otherwise I really enjoyed my time there.

Anne Browne, Bradford-on-Avon, Wilts

Anne, aged 14, in 1943

My Grandparents

My Grandfather was a gardener all his working life. His father died young, so he had to go out to work to help support his mother and sister, so missed out on much of school.

When he met and married Grandma, who was a schoolteacher, he discovered a gift for writing and became a regular gardening contributor to a popular magazine.

I would visit my grandparents on the small estate where they lived, and where Grandpa was head gardener. I'd accompany him round the garden picking fruit and vegetables, and was allowed to sample the produce – I was particularly fond of the peas!

He was an elder of the church. One Sunday when Grandfather was taking the collection, I informed the congregation in a very loud voice, 'That's my Grandpa'. I was forgiven as I was only five years old.

Their house had a large central room – kitchen, sitting room and dining room – and round the walls were shelves full of rows of bottled fruit and salted vegetables in a store cupboard. Meals were a joy, as Grandma was a very good cook.

They also had a parlour which was rarely used. There was a small organ, and a glass fronted display cabinet full of the best china and family valuables. I was allowed to admire them but never to touch.

Emily Soper, Gosport, Hants

Emily's Grandpa and Grandma

Cookery for you

BROCCOLI SALAD WITH BORLOTTI, PARSLEY, RED ONION AND TOMATO

Serves 4

- 200 g (7 oz) Broccoli, cut into 6cm (2½inch) strips
- 1 x 400 g (13 oz) tin borlotti beans, drained
- ½ red onion, sliced
- 4 ripe tomatoes, roughly chopped
- 1 small bunch of parsley shredded
- 4 tablespoons of extra virgin olive oil
- 1 tablespoon red wine vinegar
- Salt and pepper

1 Bring a medium pan of water to the boil, add the broccoli and cook for 1 minute. Drain, cool under cold running water and set aside.
2 Mix all the ingredients together, including the broccoli, in a large bowl. Season to taste and serve immediately.

Tip: Tastes great with some fresh crusty granary bread as a wholesome lunch.

Recipe courtesy Tenderstem® broccoli www.tenderstem.co.uk

Colourful climbers
Hydrangea anomala petiolaris

One of the best climbers for a north-facing wall is the climbing hydrangea. It thrives in sun or partial shade, copes with most soils and requires very little attention. Flowering between May and July it may take several years to become established, but once it has it is spectacular with massive white lacecap-style flowers. Although deciduous, the gnarled stems also look attractive and cling using adventitious roots. Height 15m. Plants widely available.

TOP TIP

If you don't like wearing gloves when gardening, put a little soap under your fingernails to prevent them getting ingrained with dirt. After gardening, scrub your nails with a brush, as usual.

Healthier for longer!

Have a drink – but go for a power walk too. Danish scientists have found that compared to tee-totallers, people who stay physically active and drink moderate amounts of alcohol have a lower risk of dying from heart disease.

THAT'S INTERESTING...

Elmer, the flying monk, leaped from Malmesbury Abbey in c1000AD in his attempt to be the first man to fly. He travelled more than a furlong but, sadly, broke both his legs.

Cookery for you

CLOUD BERRY PIMMS

Serves 1

- ◆ 35 ml (1 fl oz) Pimms
- ◆ 15 ml (¹/₂ fl oz) Hendricks Gin
- ◆ 15 ml (¹/₂ fl oz) Belvoir blueberry cordial
- ◆ 40 ml (2 fl oz) cloudy lemonade
- ◆ 20 ml (¹/₂ fl oz) cranberry juice
- ◆ Handful fresh berries and mint leaves, to serve

1 Mix all the ingredients together.
2 Put 4-5 ice cubes in a tall glass and pour in the cocktail.
3 Garnish with the fresh berries and mint leaves and serve.

Tip: To make this non-alcoholic, simply remove the gin and Pimms and double the quantity of lemonade and cranberry juice.

Recipe courtesy Belvoir Fruit Farms

My Grandparents

Above: Christine's maternal grandparents in 1950
Below: Grandfather Peter, complete with watch-chain

Between the age of 12 and 16 (1963 to 1967) I stayed with my maternal grandparents during the summer holidays because both my parents worked.

Apart from outdoor bowling, Gramps didn't have many hobbies so he taught me how to play cards. He'd be waiting for me to come downstairs each morning so I could have my tuition.

When he considered I had enough skill, we used to play for money, and before everyone recoils in horror, the money consisted of a sweet jar full of farthings. I never knew why he had so many farthings, but we used to have a lot of fun playing Newmarket, Cribbage, Pontoon, Rummy and Poker.

When I visited my paternal grandfather, it was a special treat when I was very little to sit on his lap and listen to the tick of his pocket watch, which was fastened to his waistcoat on a chain.

Christine Barrow, Plymouth, Devon

▮ THAT'S INTERESTING...

The word 'queue' is the only word in the English language that is still pronounced the same way when the last four letters are removed.

Healthier for longer!

Floss your teeth daily – avoiding gum disease could help you to live longer. The bacteria that cause gum problems also cause inflammation in your blood vessels and could harm your heart.

Colourful climbers
Wisteria sinensis

Few sights beat that of wisteria in full bloom, especially when it's growing against weathered brickwork. The purple flowers of Chinese wisteria open in early summer before the leaves appear, making an awe-inspiring sight. Like most wisterias, it may take several years to become established and becomes heavy with age, so requires plenty of support. It thrives in sun or partial shade and well-drained soils and may reach 9m in height. Plants widely available.

TOP TIP

Having trouble keeping cats off the garden? Crush some moth balls and spread them round the garden.

Mrs A E Genge, Weston-super-Mare, Avon

Meeting the stars

In 2001 my husband Robert and I went to the Cliffs Pavilion, Westcliff-on-Sea to see Lonnie Donegan – and what a great evening we had! We've been fans since we were teenagers in the 1950s and Lonnie had lost none of his magic. After the show, we queued up to get his autograph and to have a chat to him – a real gentleman with plenty of talent. We were shocked to hear of his death but have great memories of a special evening.

May Oldrey, Romford, Essex

Lonnie, putting on the style

Valerie and her brother Gerald in June 1942

Schooldays remembered

My earliest memories of Primary School in the 1940s are of gaberdine raincoats, hand-knitted pixie hoods and balaclava helmets, knitted gloves and scarves all drying out on the huge fireguard that surrounded the anthracite boiler heating our classroom. On Empire Day we would go to school carrying Union Jacks, the girls would wear red, white and blue ribbons and take flowers of the same colours, to decorate the hall. I remember we had a distribution of drinking chocolate powder and had to take a tin to school to take the powder home.

Despite my early schooling being during the war, I look back on them as happy days, and it was not until nearly the end that I realised the awful consequences. One of my schoolfriends and her family were all killed when a V2 landed on their house. Her name was Primrose and I have never forgotten her.

Valerie Bunt, Chalfont St Peter, Bucks

Schooldays remembered

Helen (with that haircut!) and her mum around 1957

Helen today, with her dad

I had a very happy time at infants and junior school in Plymouth, although I do remember having a 'wish list'.

I wished… that my name was Susan.

That I had long blonde hair, plaited, with two perfectly tied navy blue bows. (My Granddad would sit me on a stool and cut my plain brown hair with kitchen scissors, and would finish it off with blunt clippers that pulled the back of my neck – the pain!).

That I was chosen as the Fairy Queen in the school play, wearing a pink satin dress, with a silver wand. Instead, I was usually 'something in the woodland', wore a pea-green creation, black plimsolls and waved a twig about!

That I could wear black patent ankle strapped shoes to school, instead of 'sensible' shoes. But if I had to wear them, why couldn't I have steel 'Blakies' on the heels, so at least I would sound important.

That I could have a shop-bought school jumper, with a label at the back, and that was smooth and soft to the touch. Mine was a recycled hand-knitted affair – hairy, bobbly and made me itch.

That I had a bri-nylon bathing suit and soft rubber hat with flowers on. Instead I had to wear a woollen bathing suit that gravitated to the floor and weighed a ton when wet. My white bathing hat was inflexible and left a red welt around me forehead and neck that took an age to fade.

**Helen Vanstone,
Plymouth, Devon**

My Grandparents

My Grandfather was the only grandparent I remember and my visits to him entailed a bus ride, then a long walk to his house – it seemed to go on forever because my legs were so tiny. And it only became worse – no drink, no biscuit and nothing to do except melt into the walls, making sure to be quiet.

As a treat, I'd be given his moneybox, which was shaped like a bear, and would then have to count the small change that it contained.

After that, I would be allowed to sit on his lap, which I hated, so that I could be shown his pocket watch, which hung on a long chain from his pocket in his navy pinstripe waistcoat. How I longed for the visit to end so that I could go home, but first I had to endure the return journey.

Luckily, our visits were infrequent, but perhaps some good did come of it because I always plan my grandchildren's entertainment long before they arrive and we always have lots of fun! I hope their memories of me will only be good, which unhappily I can't say of the only grandparent that I knew.

**Margaret Jesson,
Bridgnorth, Shrops**

Above: Margaret's Granddad
Right: Margaret with the teddy bear moneybox

Cookery for you

PASTA WITH KALE, CHILLI & TOMATO

Serves 4

- ◆ 300 g (11 oz) dried pasta
- ◆ 200 g (7 oz) kale, shredded
- ◆ 1 tablespoon olive oil
- ◆ 1 onion, chopped
- ◆ 250 g (9 oz) smoked back bacon, chopped
- ◆ 1-2 teaspoon mild chilli powder
- ◆ 400 g (13 oz) can chopped tomatoes with herbs
- ◆ Salt and pepper
- ◆ 10 g (½ oz) Parmesan, grated to serve

1 In separate pans, boil the pasta until cooked, and kale for 10 minutes. Drain.
2 Meanwhile, heat the oil in a large frying pan and fry the onion, bacon and chilli powder for 5 minutes. Add the tomatoes and cook for 1-2 minutes.
3 Stir in the kale and pasta and season to taste. Sprinkle cheese over and serve immediately.

Recipe courtesy www,discoverkale.co.uk

THAT'S INTERESTING...

- ◆ 40% of Woman's Hour listeners are men.
- ◆ The show Educating Archie, which began in 1950, first introduced 13-year-old Julie Andrews to the radio audience.

Colourful climbers
Eccremocarpus scaber

The Chilean glory flower is an exotic-looking climber with wiry stems and sparse, evergreen leaves that are a perfect backdrop to the bright red, orange or yellow tubular flowers it produces between early summer and autumn. It grows quickly so makes useful screen, but is only hardy in sheltered regions where it dies down in winter, emerging again during the spring. In colder areas, sow seed in March and plant outside once the frost has passed.

Height 3m. Seeds widely available.

TOP TIP

Mushrooms are best stored in a paper bag in the bottom of the fridge.

Healthier for longer!

Use your imagination – according to Harvard scientists thinking creatively could help to preserve your memory. They found that people with vivid imaginations had better memory skills.

Cornwall: du Maurier Country

Smugglers' coves

Daphne du Maurier was born in London in 1907 and her life-long love affair with Cornwall began as a child when her family took their summer holidays there. The du Mauriers bought a second home, Ferryside, in the village of Bodinnick-by-Fowey and it was here that Daphne wrote her first novel, The Loving Spirit. Although the house is now privately owned, visitors are welcome at the picturesque Old Ferry Inn nearby.

During the Second World War, Daphne rented a house in Fowey, across the Helford River from Bodinnick. And in 1943 she moved from there to a romantic but neglected old house known as Menabilly which she immortalised as Manderley in one of her best-known works, Rebecca.

The whole of this historic coast and beautiful countryside inspired the author, and visitors wishing to explore further should visit The Ticket Shop and du Maurier Literary Centre at 5, South Street, Fowey where they can learn about local guided walks.

Away from south west Cornwall, standing high on Bodmin Moor, is Jamaica Inn where Daphne stayed in 1930 and used in her novel of the same name. Today, the inn, which has a room devoted to du Maurier, makes a fine base for exploring the moorland's granite tors, valleys and woods.

Closer to Fowey, other attractions include the internationally renowned Eden Project as well as the Lost Gardens of Heligan.

If Daphne du Maurier's novels have stirred an interest in Cornwall's smuggling past, you can learn more about those illicit goings-on at Charlestown Shipwreck and Heritage Centre.

Banners and bands

Ah! Happy days
Mrs Val Newman of Wrexham recalls the thrill of Whitsuntide

When I was growing up in Sheffield the Whit Walk was the highlight of the year. The night before, I was too excited to sleep. One reason for this was we were kitted out from top to toe in new clothes.

My sister and I had a new summer dress, a cardigan or jacket, a hat, and white gloves, socks and shoes. It was a matter of pride to our mothers that we were turned out well which must have meant a lot of saving.

Straight after breakfast, which we ate in our vests and knickers, in case we spilt food on our new clothes, we would get dressed and go up the street, knocking on every door, saying: "We've come to show you our new Whit clothes." The neighbours would duly admire our outfits and give us a few coppers.

Then we would race along to where the brass band was warming up outside the chapel. The minister and chapel officials were there, resplendent in their suits and shiny shoes. Our Sunday School teacher, Miss King, fussed over us, making sure we were in our proper places. The greatest honour was to walk at the head of the procession, carrying the chapel banner.

Off we went to the main road where we met groups from other chapels – a tide of banners glinting in the sun. As we approached the local park, our ranks were swelled with the Boys' Brigades, the Scouts and the May Queens on their decorated floats.

In the park our parents joined in the celebrations. On the way home, my mum would always say: "Just look at the state of your shoes and socks!"

What's in a name?

Many of our favourite stars were originally known by another name. Match the star to their birth name. If you get stuck the answers are at the bottom of the page.

PIC: REX FEATURES

1.	Woody Allen	A.	Margarita Carmen Cansino
2.	Julie Andrews	B.	Anna Maria Louisa Italiano
3.	Fred Astaire	C.	Archibald Alexander Leach
4.	Lauren Bacall	D.	Bernard Schwartz
5.	Anne Bancroft	E.	Allen Stewart Konigsberg
6.	Brigitte Bardot	F.	Ruth Elizabeth Davis
7.	Richard Burton	G.	Doris Mary Ann von Kappelhoff
8.	Michael Caine	H.	Ernest Evans
9.	Chubby Checker	I.	Frances Ethel Gumm
10.	Patsy Cline	J.	Frederick Austerlitz
11.	Joan Crawford	K.	Richard Walter Jenkins, Jr.
12.	Bing Crosby	L.	Issur Danielovitch Demsky
13.	Tony Curtis	M.	James Leblanche Stewart
14.	Doris Day	N.	Julia Elizabeth Wells
15.	Kirk Douglas	O.	Lucille Fay LeSueur
16.	Judy Garland	P.	Harry Lillis Crosby
17.	Stewart Granger	Q.	Maurice Joseph Micklewhite
18.	Cary Grant	R.	Reginald Carey Harrison
19.	Rex Harrison	S.	Betty Joan Perske
20.	Rita Hayworth	T.	Camille Javal
21.	Bette Davis	U.	Virginia Patterson Hensley

Answers: 1E, 2N, 3J, 4S, 5B, 6T, 7K, 8Q, 9H, 10U, 11O, 12P, 13D, 14G, 15L, 16I, 17M, 18C, 19R, 20A, 21F

Hang on to your hat

All Pam Clatworthy wanted to be on Empire Day was a lumberjack or an African chief but ended up feeling a proper fool...

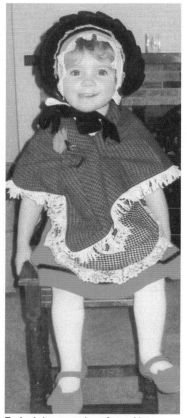
Today's improved outfit on Aimee

My neice Aimee comes running to show me her traditional Welsh costume that she will wear at the school concert. She looks beautiful and is full of pride and enthusiasm. Quite a different story from my own unfortunate experience so many years previous...

"If a teacher asks you, remember that Empire Day is held on May 24 because it was Queen Victoria's birthday – and hang on to your hat because there's a breeze getting up."

Gran closed the door on me before I could get a word in. Each day my Grandma imparted a nugget of information as I left the house for primary school. Not that any teacher ever asked, and my head is still filled with information that I've never been able to forget.

I usually enjoyed dressing-up and walking the short distance to school to perform in concerts, but today I felt a proper fool in a big, black hat and a nasty, scratchy woollen shawl.

Why did I have to be the Welsh character in a short play about children of the Empire? I wasn't a Welsh speaker and I wanted to be a Canadian lumberjack with an axe, or an African chief holding a cocoa pod, but only boys could do that.

'Cymru am byth', I had to say. 'I come from Wales and bring coal to fuel the engines of the empire'.

I clung on to my enormous hat as I ambled into the playground. The hat was black, shiny and weighed a ton. Can you imagine wearing a tall tower made of layers of old newspapers stuck together with Gloy, and painted with stovepipe black, then varnished? The frilly inside cap was yellowing paper doilies searched out from the wardrobe and which stank of old cigars and mothballs. I felt an absolute ninny.

We all stood to attention as the headmaster hoisted the Union Flag. He'd been a soldier in the First World War and it was all too much for him. He wept as the school choir sang the national anthem. Our music teacher sat at the upright piano wheeled outside for the occasion. She thumped away while trying to hang on to sheets of music as they fluttered in the morning breeze.

We prayed for King George, the government, colonies, dominions and empire, then for our brave troops wherever they might be. Then it was time for the play. Thankfully I remember little about it, except how embarrassed I felt. The large piece of Welsh anthracite gleaming with an application of floor polish made my hands black. I stammered on my unfamiliar words but nobody

Why did I have to be the Welsh character in a short play

You can't miss Pam and that hat – back row, third from left

sniggered, I'd got away with it.

Unfortunately, I had to stand next to my friendly enemy Heather. She was a feisty lass and we sometimes almost came to blows at playtime. She represented Scotland and was perfectly kitted out in every detail. Her bonnet fitted well, her kilt was the authentic clan tartan and she looked so good. How I hated Heather that morning.

Out of sight in the school shrubbery I tried to squash my dreadful hat

Full of envy I wanted to grab her packet of porridge oats and pour them over her glossy red curls.

We sang Jerusalem, had prayers led by the vicar, the Last Post played by the Boys' Brigade bugler, stood to attention for the Welsh national anthem, and then it was time to go home.

O ut of sight in the school shrubbery I tried to squash my dreadful hat – to no avail. Despite jumping on it, the hat remained as firm as the Rock of Gibraltar. With great venom, I kicked it into the school air-raid shelter, chucked the coal after it and ran to join my friends.

It took a long time to get home, the sow at Cutters Farm had just delivered some fine piglets and my itchy shawl caught

on a nail as I peered into the sty. I deliberately ripped into the weakened fabric. Another piece of my hated costume was now destroyed forever.

My Gran was sitting at the kitchen table reading the newspaper when I eventually got home. "Did it go well?" she asked. "Where's your hat?"

"Oh it collapsed," I said. "It wasn't worth bringing home. My shawl's torn too." "Pity," she said. 'They would have come in handy for next year.'

Oh no, I thought. Not likely. Never again. Never, ever. If I can't be a lumberjack, I'll run away from home.

The following year I landed up in hospital with scarlet fever, so my acting career came to an abrupt end…

June 2009

Monday
1

Tuesday
2
Anniversary of **HM** Queen Elizabeth II's coronation

Wednesday
3

Thursday
4

Friday
5

Saturday
6
Epsom Derby

Sunday
7

Monday
8

Tuesday
9

Wednesday
10

Thursday
11

Friday
12

Saturday
13

Sunday
14

Monday
15

Tuesday
16

Wednesday
17

Thursday
18

Friday
19

Saturday
20

Sunday
21
Father's Day

Monday
22

Tuesday **23**	Saturday **27**
Wednesday **24**	Sunday **28**
Thursday **25**	Monday **29**
Friday **26**	Tuesday **30**

Behind the Scenes

Funny Lady, 1975

Blonde ringlets and a very large fetching bow – not a hairstyle you'd immediately associate with superstar Barbra Streisand – but she's in costume as she films the 1975 movie Funny Girl. She doesn't look too worried as she sits and talks to the film's director, Herbert Ross.

Director and actress had worked together frequently, with Ross as choreographer on Barbra's first Broadway musical, I Can Get It For You Wholesale, in 1962, and on the saucy 1970 film The Owl and the Pussycat. Ross also choreographed Cliff Richard's two 1960s musicals, The Young Ones and Summer Holiday.

Funny Lady was a sequel to

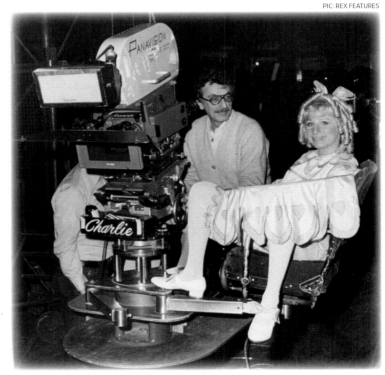

Funny Girl, Streisand returning to the role which put her on the map, that of comedienne and singer Fanny Brice who, at the beginning of Funny Lady, has divorced her first husband, Nicky Arnstein. She starred with James Caan as Fanny's second husband, songwriter and entrepreneur, Billy Rose.

Funny Lady featured the songs More Than You Know, It's Only a Paper Moon, Am I Blue? and So Long, Honey Lamb.

Cookery for you

BANANA, PLUM, SULTANA & APRICOT BUTTERY FLAPJACKS

Makes approx 28

- ◆ 275 g (10 oz) rolled porridge oats
- ◆ 1 medium banana, peeled and thinly sliced
- ◆ 2 small plums, stoned and cut into small pieces
- ◆ 25 g (1 oz) dried apricots, chopped
- ◆ 25 g (1 oz) sultanas
- ◆ 225 g (8 oz) Anchor Lighter Spreadable
- ◆ 175 g (6 oz) Demerara sugar
- ◆ 75 g (3 oz) golden syrup

1 Preheat the oven to 160°C/325°F/Gas Mark 3. In a large bowl mix together the oats, banana, plums, apricots and sultanas.

2 In a small saucepan place the Anchor Lighter Spreadable, sugar and syrup and melt gently together.

3 Gradually pour the melted syrupy mixture onto the oats, and stir together until all ingredients are well coated.

4 Spoon into a non-stick, or greased and lined, 30cm x 20cm x 2 ½cm tin (12in x 8in x 1in tin) and flatten out mixture until smoothed into all the corners of the tray.

5 Place in the oven for 25-30 minutes, or until the mixture is golden brown.

6 Remove from oven and allow to cool a little before cutting into squares while still warm – store in an airtight container.

Recipe courtesy Anchor butter, www.freerangebutter.co.uk

My Grandparents

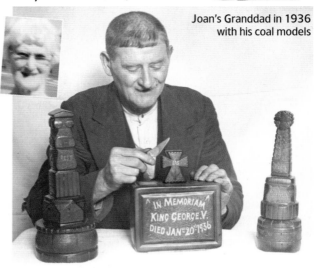

Joan's Granddad in 1936 with his coal models

My Granddad, Tom Walker, was born in Elsecar in 1867, and worked as a miner until he had to give up due to ill health. After he gave up work he started carving models from coal, using only a knife and a small file.

Every summer during and just after the war I spent two weeks of my school holiday with him and his daughter – my beloved Auntie Norah, in their miner's cottage.

I used to sit watching him, fascinated, as he carved and smoothed lumps of coal into the most beautiful shapes – memorials, boots, shoes, Bibles. He would sit in a corner near the fire with a leather apron across his knees, patiently working, hardly saying a word.

His other passion was his allotment – he would take my hand and we would go up there, where he showed me how to sow seeds, plant and weed. He also told me about birds and butterflies which were frequent visitors.

When I was young, I was a little afraid of him, but soon learned that under that stern exterior was a warm-hearted loving man.

I always had a magical time with him and my Aunt, and was sorry to go home, and would count the weeks until it was time to visit them again.

Joan Morton, Retford, Notts

THAT'S INTERESTING...

The average British citizen is caught on CCTV around 300 times a day.

Colourful climbers
Trachelospermum jasminoides

One of the best of all garden climbers, this woody evergreen produces rich, dark green leaves that turn bronze in winter. During summer, white flowers that smell wonderfully of jasmine cover the plant, making it a joy to behold. It thrives in well-drained soils in sun or partial shade but requires protection from cold, drying winds. It reaches 9m in height. Plants widely available.

TOP TIP
When packing a suitcase to go on holiday, use tissue paper to keep your clothes crease free.

Meeting the stars

I met Carol Klein at RHS Chelsea Flower Show in 1999, the year she had a plot for a cottage garden outside the marquee – I believe it was the first time she'd exhibited there.

I was there because I'd organised a stand for a charity supporting education for blind and sight-impaired children and students. When we'd finished our hard work, we took our cameras to look out for visiting celebrities.

I'm very interested in gardening, so I was thrilled to meet Carol. Now I've retired, I have much more time for my garden, and keeping up with Carol and her wonderful enthusiasm for horticulture.   **Drina Brokenbrow, High Wycombe, Bucks**

Drina meeting Carol Klein

Healthier for longer!
Sprinkle on blueberries – they're packed with flavonoids called anthocyanins which could help to reduce your risk of heart disease, cancer, improve your eye sight and slow down the ageing process inside and out.

Schooldays remembered

Josephine in 1944

During the war in London, if you had siblings at school already then we could attend at three years old, which I did. I remember classes being disrupted because of the air raids. Sometimes school lunches were provided and these were long sandwich loaves delivered on big wooden trays. I can recall the taste of the wonderful bread!

School ended at about 3.30pm (a long day for a three-year-old) but we were never sure we'd have a home to go back to. Somehow, we coped.

Josephine Masters, Tenterden, Kent

Cookery for you

Colourful climbers
Pineapple broom

The Moroccan shrub Cytisus battandieri may have proved hardier than predicted, but still grows best against a sunny south-facing wall with shelter from cold winds. It makes an excellent wall shrub, with silky grey-green leaves that contrast effectively with rustic brickwork. In summer, golden pea-shaped flowers are produced that smell strongly of pineapples. It enjoys well-drained soils and may reach 5m in height. Plants widely available.

BROCCOLI SALAD WITH CRACKED WHEAT, PISTACHIO AND APRICOTS

Serves 4

- 110 g (4 oz) broccoli cut into 5cm (2in) strips
- 110 g (4 oz) cracked wheat
- 50 g (2 oz) pistachios, roughly chopped
- 50 g (2 oz) apricots, chopped
- 1 small red onion, chopped
- Small bunch mint, shredded
- Small bunch parsley, shredded
- 1 lemon, grated and juice
- 4 tablespoons extra virgin olive oil
- Salt and cracked black pepper

1 Bring a small pan of water to the boil. Add the broccoli and cook for 1 minute. Drain, cool under cold running water and then set aside.
2 Boil a kettle and in a medium-sized bowl add the cracked wheat. When the kettle has boiled, cover the cracked wheat with boiling water, cling film the bowl and leave for 30 minutes.
3 After 30 minutes, drain off any excess water from the cracked wheat.
4 Add all the other ingredients, season with the salt and pepper and serve immediately.

Recipe courtesy Tenderstem® broccoli, www.tenderstem.co.uk

Healthier for longer!

Get walking – for good health you should be clocking up 10,000 steps a day. Invest in a pedometer – available from good sports shops – to help you make sure you're doing enough.

THAT'S INTERESTING...

'Carpet bagger': A candidate who has no interest in the constituency he represents.

Original meaning: A Unionist financier who exploited the cheap labour available in the South after the American Civil War. The bags carried by these people were often made of carpet.

Georgina with her grandparents

My Grandparents

On the way to the Nore lightship

I recall a holiday spent with my grandparents and aunt at Westcliff-on-Sea, the picnics on the beach, the delicious sandwiches with succulent ham and new bread, which we didn't have at home.

One evening we went by motorboat to view the Nore lightship. It was chilly and someone on the boat lent me a cardigan which you'll see from the photograph was rather too big for me.

When we reached the lightship I clambered aboard with some others from the boat, and climbed a rope ladder to watch the huge lantern flash on and off out to sea.

The trouble started when I had to go down the ladder backwards. I simply couldn't bring myself to do this and no one could persuade me.

When I was the last on the ship, a sailor arrived. He climbed the ladder, turned me round and stood up very close to me on the ladder and took each foot in turn and placed it on a rung until we got to the bottom and I was handed back to my grandparents and everyone waiting patiently on the boat.

I often wonder what became of the Nore lightship; I imagine it has been replaced by something modern – I would be interested to know.

Georgina Padwick,
Worthing, West Sussex

Schooldays remembered

Muriel aged about eight

I was born in 1921, and owing to poor health, I wasn't allowed to go to school until I was seven. I could read and write by the time I went, but what a shock it turned out to be; I'd been at home with my Mother and was quite used to playing by myself.

The Methodist school had three classrooms with an open fire in each which had fireguards in front. No school dinners, so we took sandwiches and a flask. The boys were rude and chased the girls, running about with food in our hands. I just hated it.

My mother went to see the headmistress and I was allowed to have my sandwiches with her in her house next door to the school. Then a friend of one of my brothers' was told to look after me, then life was a bit more pleasant.

At 11, my parents decided enough was enough and I was sent to Hastings to a private school and from then on life was great. My history mistress encouraged me as I'd always loved history and literature, and it was like a new opening in my life.

Muriel Green,
Tiverton, Devon

Cookery for you

HAZELNUT AND SULTANA COOKIES

Makes: 20

◆ 250 g (9 oz) sultanas
◆ 75 g (3 oz) unsalted butter, cut into small pieces
◆ 75 g (3 oz) brown self-raising flour
◆ 110 g (4 oz) oatmeal
◆ 110 g (4 oz) hazelnuts, toasted and roughly chopped
◆ 75 g (3 oz) light muscovado sugar
◆ Icing sugar, for dusting

1 Preheat the oven to 200°C/400°F/Gas Mark 6 and grease 2 baking sheets.
2 Put 150g (5 oz) of the sultanas in a small saucepan with 75 ml (3 fl oz) water. Bring to the boil, reduce the heat to a simmer and cook gently for 5 minutes until the sultanas are plump and the water is absorbed.
3 Tip into a food processor and add the butter. Blend until smooth.
4 Sift the flour into a bowl, tipping in any grain left in the sieve. Stir in the oatmeal, hazelnuts, sugar and remaining sultanas. Mix well then add the sultana purée and mix to a thick paste.
5 Take dessertspoonfuls of the mixture and shape roughly into 20 rounds. Place on the baking sheets and flatten slightly. Bake for 12 minutes or until slightly risen. Transfer to a wire rack to cool, then lightly dust with icing sugar.

Recipe courtesy www.allaboutoats.com

My Grandparents

Peace, perfect peace for Sandra's grandparents

This photograph of my grandparents, David and Hilda, always makes me smile. It was taken at Butlins, 1951, in Wales by the local camp photographer. They had fallen asleep on a warm sunny afternoon and had a surprise on seeing themselves up on the camp's photo board. I was five at the time.

It was such a lovely holiday, and I can remember certain things very clearly. The loud music as we walked down for our meals, playing on bronco horses in the playroom with my cousin Jan; Mum and Dad wearing swimming costumes and laughing a lot; watching a lady lion tamer with a real lion and making him perform in a field.

Sandra Rowan, Ellesmere Port, Cheshire

TOP TIP

To make wine glasses sparkle, rinse in cold water with a dash of vinegar.

THAT'S INTERESTING...

'If you've never seen a total eclipse, just watch a groom at a wedding…'

**Herbert V Prochnow,
American banker and toastmaster**

Schooldays remembered

My schooldays growing up in 1930s Ireland were like most other children – I never seemed to worry about anything, just so long as my homework was done and I'd learned my times tables.

I was taught by nuns, and we had a bottle of milk in the morning and a mug of soup in the afternoon. It wasn't until years later that I discovered it was only 'poor' children who got the soup – but I certainly never thought of myself as poor.

One day, as we were queuing for our soup, someone noticed a dead mouse floating in the big saucepan – you can imagine the uproar!

Being 10 at the time, I knew a mouse wasn't one of the ingredients my mother used when she was making soup. Our nun didn't turn a hair, she just lifted the mouse on the soup ladle and said in a gentle voice, 'Would you look at the poor wee laddie. He must have wanted a taste of this delicious soup and fell in. We'll bury him later, shall we children?' That's just what we did - after we'd finished the soup, of course!

Christina Kelly, Worcester

Healthier for longer!

Make steak a treat – eating too much red and processed meats such as sausages could increase your risk of certain cancers say experts at the US National Cancer Institute. Don't cut it out altogether though – a lean steak is an excellent source of iron.

Meeting the stars

This photograph of Peter Noone from Herman's Hermits and Davy Jones from the Monkees was taken when my brother David and nephew Ian went to a concert in California and were invited backstage afterwards to meet them.

Pearl Landragin, London SE12

Peter Noone and Davy Jones with David and Ian

Colourful climbers
Ampelopsis brevipedunculata 'Elegans'

Ampelopsis is great in a small garden because its stems die down each winter, ensuring it always remains compact. It has pink, cream and green variegated leaves that contrast attractively with the dark pink tendrils by which it climbs. Small gemlike turquoise fruits may be produced in sunny years. Cut back the stems in late autumn. It thrives in full sun or partial shade and loves a moist well-drained soil, reaching 5m in height. Plants widely available.

Schooldays remembered

Seven-year-old Sylvia

My very first day at school in 1950 is still etched indelibly in my mind. My older sister Joan likened the first sighting of me during that inital playtime as, 'Looking like a rabbit caught in car headlights' as I clung, terrified, to the playground railings. I was a shy child, so the first few weeks took some getting used to.

Morning break meant small bottles of milk, warm and on the turn in the summer, and frozen hard in the winter, with at least two inches of ice above the bottle. One classroom had a stove that burnt coke, which made the room very hot and gave off a fuggy smell – I was always ready to doze off.

I had a very hearty appetite and loved school dinners, especially the chocolate semolina pudding; the other children on my table didn't like it, so I was happy to have their share. I loved cabbage at home, but school cabbage had bicarb in it, so it was bitter, as was the pig's liver.

We did PE in all weathers – I really hated getting into PE knickers as I was so skinny throughout my schooldays and I was picked on mercilessly. My nickname was 'Sticks' or 'broomsticks' (my surname was Broomer).

I enjoyed netball in secondary school but as all my friends were developing curves, and I was still a beanpole, the thought of shorts flapping around my long skinny legs made me even more self conscious. I still cringe to this day when I recall wearing a pair my mum made for me, from a pair of old curtains!

**Sylvia Washington,
Wellington, Somerset**

My Grandparents

My Grannie and Granddad Williams were of the generation who believed that children should be seen and not heard, and that they should only speak when spoken to. Grannie was always very upright and sat on a straight back chair.

When we visited I had to sit on a dining chair and not slouch, not swing my legs, and not fidget.

At tea time no elbows were allowed on the table and the only time I spoke was to say, 'yes please' or 'no thank you'. So it is not surprising that I did not look forward to our fortnightly visits, and when I reached my early teens, I found excuses not to go.

Looking back now, I feel guilty and I realise what good training it was to have good manners, but I do wish my grandparents had been more relaxed and more fun, as we try to be with our grandchildren.

**Barbara Cox, Hexham,
Northumberland**

Grannie and Granddad Williams

Cookery for you

CHILLED POTATO & AVOCADO SOUP

Serves 4

- ◆ 1 tablespoon olive oil
- ◆ 1 onion, chopped
- ◆ ¹/₂ teaspoon chilli flakes
- ◆ 2 floury potatoes, (approx 450 g/1 lb), peeled and diced
- ◆ 1 litre (1³/₄ pints) vegetable stock
- ◆ 2 ripe avocados
- ◆ 170 ml carton soured cream
- ◆ Chopped coriander, to garnish

1 Heat the olive oil in a large saucepan and fry the onion for 5-6 minutes over a gentle heat.
2 Add the chilli and fry for 2-3 minutes. Add the potatoes and stock. Bring to the boil and simmer, covered for 10 minutes until tender.
3 Using a hand-held blender or food processor, blend the soup until smooth and allow to cool. Add the avocado and soured cream and blend again, season to taste.
4 Chill before serving, garnish with the chopped coriander.

Tip: Potatoes and avocados are a classic Peruvian combination. This soup is a delicious chilled twist on the traditional potato and avocado soup found all across South America, and makes a great unusual starter.

Recipe courtesy the British Potato Council

Colourful climbers
Humulus lupulus 'Aureus'

The golden hop is a spectacular climber that will twine prettily through trellis, over obelisks and through trees. It thrives in full sun but retains more of its luscious lime-green colour when grown in partial shade. It copes with most soil types and may reach 5m in height. However, it should be cut hard back every spring, as the fresh new growth is the most attractive. Plants widely available.

THAT'S INTERESTING...

The heat wave of 1976 began in earnest on June 23, and for 14 consecutive days the temperature topped 32°C at a number of places in southern England.

TOP TIP

A couple of sugar lumps kept in a dry Thermos flask will keep it fresh when not in use.
Florrie Harvey, Stoke-on-Trent, Staffs

Healthier for longer!

Wear sunglasses – protect your eyes from ageing UV damage by investing in a good pair of sunglasses. Make sure they have a label that says they have a UV filter and wear them whenever the sun is shining.

Dorset: Thomas Hardy Country

Wonderful Wessex

The cottage in Higher Bockhampton where Thomas Hardy was born in June 1840 is now owned by The National Trust and makes a good starting point for exploring the author's beloved Dorset. It was in the bedroom of this picture-book cottage that he wrote his first four novels, including Far from the Madding Crowd.

Apart from five years spent in London, Hardy resided most of his life in Dorset which appears in his books as part of the imaginary county of Wessex. Egdon Heath, the brooding backdrop to The Return of the Native, is based on the two heaths of Tincleton and Bere.

Many of the county's towns appear in his novels under other names: the pretty town of Bere Regis became Kingsbere in Tess of the D'Urbervilles and Dorchester, where he went to school, became Casterbridge in The Mayor of Casterbridge.

A mile outside Dorchester is another National Trust property, Max Gate, the house that Hardy designed himself (he had trained as an architect) and where he lived until his death in 1928.

Although Thomas Hardy's ashes are interred in Westminster Abbey's Poets' Corner, his heart is buried in the churchyard of St Michael's in Stinsford where his family worshipped. A stained glass window is inscribed in his honour.

Other attractions include the formal Edwardian garden and ornamental lake at Kingston Maurward where there is an animal park with miniature Shetland ponies and donkeys.

A fine romance

My drummer boy

It was love at first sight for Mrs Flo Carvell of Rainham, Essex

It was towards the end of 1954 that my friend at work, Millie, asked me to a party that was being given for her brother who was home on leave from serving with the Forces in Germany.

When we arrived at the party it was already quite crowded but I immediately spied a fellow in a corner playing the drums. I said to the girl who had come with me: "I don't care what Millie's brother is like, I fancy him on the drums."

Imagine my surprise when I was introduced to Millie's brother and he WAS the fellow on the drums! We dated while he was on leave, then wrote to each other. After six weeks we got engaged and were married when he was demobbed.

I wrote a short poem that I feel is very apt for us.

He is Les, I am Flo,
How it will work, I don't know.
I have a temper; so has he.
Oh, what a marriage ours will be!
Somehow, though, I think we may
Get along in our own queer way,
For each has something more than pride;
A love that just cannot be denied.

They said it wouldn't last but we proved them wrong and have now been married over 52 years. We go dancing every week, jiving and bopping – and we never let the sun go down on our quarrels.

And the budgie came too

Half the fun of holidaying in the 1950s, remembers Maureen Smith, was the challenge of getting there...

When my sister and I were small, our holidays were generally spent in a caravan at Talybont in North Wales,

Although the holiday itself was pretty straightforward as caravan holidays go in the 1950s – we would build sandcastles, paddle in the sea and go for walks along the 'Fairy Glen', we had far more adventures attempting to get there in the first place!

My father and my uncle both had motorcycle combinations – a motorbike with a sidecar for carrying passengers. We'd travel in convoy (eventually) to our destination.

However, my uncle had to come from Birmingham and we'd set off from Lichfield and arrange to meet at a certain point en route, where we'd all have a bacon and egg breakfast on the roadside, cooked on a primus stove.

But we'd invariably meet up way before then, since my father nearly always managed to get a puncture and my uncle would come across us while my dad was repairing it. It was a known fact that my mother seemed to push the motorcycle combination as many miles as she appeared to ride on it!

I should point out that when we went on holiday we always took Timmy, our budgerigar with us – we couldn't bear to leave him with anyone else. My sister would be in the front seat of the sidecar with the suitcase between her legs. This must have been uncomfortable because it was a long journey and she'd be unable to move her position much as space was limited.

And with even less space in the 'dicky' seat (built on as an extension by my father), I'd have the budgie in his cage on my lap. This too, could prove dicey as the roads were quite bumpy and motorbikes aren't so smooth in the suspension as cars. The poor budgie frequently fell off his perch and struggled to hang on most of the time!

Maureen's mum and sister, Pat, watching Dad mend a puncture

The other problem we had to contend with was my father's penchant for getting lost. (I'm sure my sense of direction is inherited from him.) We'd been known to go round many an island several times, and on one occasion when a policeman was directing the traffic, his mouth fell open when he saw us sailing by again, with the poor budgie in the back hanging on for grim death.

Although my father used to take a lot of stick from my uncle about our problems with punctures and getting lost, we did, on one occasion, have a good laugh at his and my aunt's expense.

We were travelling along one day in convoy and came round a corner, and suddenly heard my aunt yelling at the top of her voice behind us. You had to yell really loudly, since it was difficult to hear anything through the crash helmets we wore, with the wind whizzing by.

We eventually slowed down and found out that the bottom had fallen out of their sidecar and my aunt's rear had been bouncing on the road. This must have been awful for her, but my sister and I were helpless with laughter. It just so happened that there were a group of soldiers standing nearby and they, too, were highly amused! After that experience my aunt refused to go in the sidecar ever again.

July 2009

Wednesday

1

Thursday

2

Friday

3

Saturday

4

American Independence Day

Sunday

5

Monday

6

Tuesday

7

Wednesday

8

Thursday

9

Friday

10

Saturday

11

Sunday

12

Monday

13

Battle of the Boyne (Bank Holiday, N Ireland)

Tuesday

14

Wednesday

15

St Swithun's Day

Thursday

16

Friday

17

Saturday

18

Sunday

19

Monday

20

Tuesday

21

Wednesday

22

Thursday **23**	Tuesday **28**
Friday **24**	Wednesday **29**
Saturday **25**	Thursday **30**
Sunday **26**	Friday **31**
Monday **27**	

PIC: REX FEATURES

Behind the Scenes

My Fair Lady, 1964

Time for a spruce up and a quick cup of tea for Rex Harrison on the film set of 1964's My Fair Lady, as Wilfred Hyde-White (left) and Stanley Holloway (right) look on.

Based on George Bernard Shaw's Pygmalion, everyone knows the story – (and the Lerner and Loewe songs) – of Professor Higgins and his protégée Eliza Doolittle. But after Mary Martin had declined the stage role of Eliza, it was Julie Andrews who triumphed on stage, Audrey Hepburn then taking on the film role, her singing voice dubbed by Marni Nixon.

Wilfred Hyde-White had shown his acting pedigree as the roguish Soapy Stevens in Two Way Stretch (1960) with Peter Sellers, and was equally at home with upper class roles such as Colonel Pickering, Professor Higgins' fellow linguist. Stanley Holloway was renowned for his comic songs and monologues – especially The Lion and Albert – and turned in a rousing 'Get Me To The Church On Time' performance as Albert Doolittle.

My Grandparents

My Grandma (Gram) lived in Sheffield, and was left a widow at 38, with six children, my dad being the eldest. I was the first grandchild, and was idolised from the start (spoilt, my mum always said).

I spent all my school holidays at Gram's. The kettle was always boiling for tea, and the wireless always on – Music While You Work, Mrs Dale's Diary, Workers' Playtime, Woman's Hour, and sometimes dancing tunes, and Gram would say, 'Come on, Shirl, this is a barn dance', and we'd have a little twirl.

On Tuesday and Thursday we'd go to the first half pictures at the Ritz. Gram's garden grew rhubarb and

Grandma and Shirley in 1939

strawberries, also fruit trees, enough to play Tarzan or cowboys, depending on which film we'd seen that week!

Shirley Berrisford, Sheffield

Colourful climbers
Cobaea scandens

Also called 'cups and saucers', this beautiful climber hails from Mexico and is only half-hardy. However, the large bell-like velvety blue flowers it produces make it an essential element of every garden. Sow the seed in spring and plant the seedlings outside when all danger of frost has passed. It thrives in full sun and may reach 6m in height. Seeds widely available.

Cookery for you

APRICOT AND ALMOND SLICE
Makes 8 slices

- ◆ 110 g (4 oz) rolled oats
- ◆ 150 g (5 oz) flaked almonds
- ◆ 2 teaspoons baking powder
- ◆ 110 g (4 oz) golden caster sugar, plus 2 teaspoons to sprinkle
- ◆ 2 medium eggs, beaten
- ◆ 2 pieces stem ginger from a jar, chopped
- ◆ 150 g (5 oz) soft dried apricots, roughly chopped

1 Preheat the oven to 180°C/350°F/Gas Mark 4. Grease a 450 g (1 lb) loaf tin and line with greaseproof paper.
2 Blend 50 g (2 oz) of oats in food processor until finely ground. Tip into a bowl. Blend half the flaked almonds until ground and add to the bowl with all but 2 tablespoons of the remaining flaked almonds; the rolled oats, baking powder and caster sugar.
3 Mix the eggs with the stem ginger and 75 ml (3 fl oz) cold water. Add to the bowl with the chopped apricots. Mix well, then turn into the tin and scatter with the reserved almonds. Bake for 30-35 minutes or until golden and just firm to the touch. Loosen the cake at the ends of the tin then lift out onto a wire rack. Sprinkle with the remaining sugar and leave to cool. Serve thinly sliced.

Recipe courtesy www.allaboutoats.com

Schooldays remembered

From Primary School during the war years, I remember lessons in the Anderson shelter during the air raids. We'd sit on benches, with the teacher in the middle, recite our tables and do mental arithmetic.

When I was 12 I moved to Ashford Grammar School, and in the 6th form the Music Club productions were great. My main interests were in Librarian work and being a prefect – both prepared me for teaching.

**Priscilla Odell,
Hampton, Middx**

Below: Gwen in Primary School days
Left: Jean in Grammar School uniform (1955)

Healthier for longer!

Get gardening – indulging in a bit of light weeding and digging a couple of times a week and then tucking into a green salad four or more times a week, could help you significantly reduce your risk of lung cancer. The salad gives you essential nutrients and the gardening works your heart and lungs.

THAT'S INTERESTING...

The estimated number of Personal Computers (PCs) in use by the year 2010 is 1.3 billion.

Meeting the stars

As a professional guitarist, I accompanied many famous singers. Before I joined the Karl Denver Trio, I worked with Tessie O'Shea at the Cabaret Club in Manchester. After working on cruise liners, I joined a band, working with my favourite star, Eartha Kitt. She'd arrived from Beverley Hills, and after standing on her head in the bandroom on the first day of rehearsals, she asked where the nearest fish and chip shop was. We all had a tasty supper thanks to Eartha! And in the words of her famous song, 'Just an old fashioned girl' she was just that – and a great lady, too!

**Brian Horton, Caerphilly,
Mid Glamorgan**

Right: Tessie in full swing with Brian (left)
Below: Eartha with the boys. Brian's peeping over her shoulder

Schooldays remembered

Wendy and I met in 1950 when we started at the local grammar school, and very soon we were inseparable. I don't know whether she was more accident prone than I was but we always seemed to be in some trouble or other.

We both loathed hockey, so welcomed the rain which meant ballroom dancing in the hall instead. I always took the man's part which was fine until, years later, when I went to dances I would try to lead my gentleman partner!

What a pair we were in housecraft. On one occasion while we were one each side of an electric stove, Wendy surreptitiously passed me a sweet, which she proceeded to drop on the hot plate. She frantically tried to scoop it up, giving herself a large blister on her index finger. And she was immediately found out as it was a mint, so the smell wafted around the room.

My Cookery O level practical exam was dreadful; I had to cook a 'menu for an invalid' ... fish in a sauce and beef tea.

I'd never done this in class so I decided to put the fish in between two plates on a saucepan of water, then went onto the beef tea. I completely forgot about the fish until one of the girls came up to me in tears and said my saucepan had melted over her cabbage!

Much to my horror, the saucepan water had evaporated and the base had melted over the cabbage which she'd left underneath the hob to keep warm.

Wendy, poor soul, had had to bake biscuits which she managed to burn. She put them in her apron pocket and every time she passed, gave me one to eat as a way of getting rid of them!

Elizabeth Howell, Port Talbot, Neath

Wendy (left) and Elizabeth in 1956

My Grandparents

Joy's grandparents, Alice and Charley Halsey

Every Saturday afternoon, my mother would take my brother and myself to Hitchin to visit our grandparents for tea. On the way we'd stop at the fishmongers to buy Granddad a pint of winkles. Tea was a big occasion, with crumpets, sandwiches and cakes but the real highlight of the tea came when Granddad got out his winkle pin to eat his winkles.

My brother and I waited with bated breath until he'd had a few winkles, then our turn was so exciting. He'd laughingly give us one each, then we'd wait for our turn to come round again. I'll never forget Saturdays and the winkles!

Joy Gyford, Lower Cambourne, Cambs

Cookery for you

POTATO, PEA AND TROUT SALAD WITH POACHED EGG

Serves 4

- ◆ 350 g (12 oz) baby new potatoes, halved
- ◆ 200 g (7 oz) freshly podded peas
- ◆ 4 spring onions, finely sliced
- ◆ 2 tablespoons olive oil
- ◆ Zest and juice of 1 lemon
- ◆ 2 tablespoons chopped fresh parsley
- ◆ 200 g (7 oz) hot smoked trout
- ◆ 145 g (5 oz) mixed watercress spinach and rocket leaves
- ◆ 4 medium eggs

1 Cook the potatoes in boiling salted water for 8 minutes, or until just tender. Add the peas and boil for a further 2 mins. Drain, then place in a large bowl.

2 Add the spring onions, olive oil, lemon zest and juice, and parsley and toss together. Season to taste. Add the trout and set aside.

3 Boil a large pan of water and set to simmer. Carefully crack in the eggs and poach for 3-4 minutes.

4 While the eggs cook, add the leaves to the warm salad and lightly toss together. Divide between four plates. Remove the eggs from the hot water with a slotted spoon and place on top of the salad. Serve immediately.

Recipe courtesy UK Salad Producers

Colourful climbers
Rhodochiton atrosanguineus

Although this climber is only half-hardy, it's so popular that you can often find it in garden centres from May onwards. The blooms, which are a wonderful combination of pink and deep purple, are produced abundantly during the summer, ensuring it looks wonderful on archways, trellis or obelisks. It's best grown as an annual by sowing seed during March and may reach 3m in height. Seeds widely available.

TOP TIP

If you're on a walking holiday, line the inside of your rucksack with a bin liner and tie it up, to keep the contents dry if it rains.

Healthier for longer!

Read a good book – spare half an hour to curl up with your favourite book, it's self defence for your brain. Studies show that bookworms outperform people with lower reading levels on cognitive tests.

THAT'S INTERESTING...

The Sun is, at present, about 70% hydrogen and 28% helium by mass. Everything else (metals) amounts to less than 2%. This changes slowly over time as the Sun converts hydrogen to helium in its core.

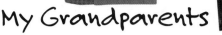

Cookery for you

LAVENDER ICE CREAM

Serves 6-8

- ◆ 570 ml (1 pint) Gold Top milk
- ◆ 10 sprigs of fresh lavender
- ◆ 4 medium egg yolks
- ◆ 175 g (6 oz) runny honey
- ◆ 284 ml (¹/₂ pint) pot double cream

1 In a medium saucepan, heat the milk until it starts simmering, add the lavender sprigs and leave to infuse for 30 minutes.

2 In a bowl, whisk the egg yolks and honey together until thick. Strain the milk into the bowl and mix well.

3 Pour the mixture back into the saucepan over a gentle heat and stir to make a smooth custard which coats the back of a wooden spoon. Strain again into a large bowl and leave to cool, then place in the fridge until chilled.

4 Whip the cream and fold into the custard. Pour the mixture into a plastic container and freeze until the sides begin to set, then remove from the freezer and stir mixture well. Freeze again until almost frozen, then stir again, cover and return to the freezer.

5 Before serving, place the container in the fridge for 10-15 minutes to let it soften.

6 Serve with raspberries.

Recipe courtesy Gold Top milk, www.gold-top.co.uk

My Grandparents

Granddad Robert and Nannie Louisa Morley, with Barbara and little Shirley

Nannie and Granddad played a big part in my early life, and each winter they would buy me a matching coat and hat, and every Friday night my Grandfather and aunts each had to contribute one penny to a saving box to pay for my new shoes.

Nan made me summer dresses; we went to a drapery shop in Tooting which had shelves packed with rolls of material – Hawkins 'Miss Muffet Prints', a favourite with little girls, advertised as being 'Direct from the Mills'. Nan bought two yards at 6d a yard, and I had a new dress with matching knickers for one shilling.

I remember particularly going on holiday with them to Winchelsea in 1936. Our accommodation was an old railway carriage, divided into three.

The first part had a washing up bowl and primus, sliding doors leading to a compartment with long side cushions and a table, the third part had a double bed, which I shared with my aunt and nine-month-old cousin, Shirley. My grandparents slept on a converted bed in the living room.

In the photograph, I was wearing a red and white check sundress and jacket which my grandmother had made. The swimming hat was because I had a large dressing on my left ear, suffering from earache after a bout of measles.

Barbara Parke, Lingfield, Surrey

Schooldays remembered

My first recollections are of infants school, and the highlight of the morning at five years old being the daily drink of milk – with paper straws that went very soggy very quickly!

We would also bring a snack with us, biscuits or cold buttered toast wrapped in greaseproof. The snacks were religiously put in a hanging blanket of small pockets, each with our name on. The smell of cold toast always

Jeanette in a party dress

reminds me of those first days at school.

Jeanette Styles, Gloucester, Glos

Healthier for longer!

Get a trainer – make an appointment for a personal training session at your local gym. A qualified trainer will help you work out the best fitness routine for you, give you realistic goals to work towards and will check up on your progress.

TOP TIP

To stop bananas going brown too quickly, wrap them in foil and put them in the fridge.

Mrs M Moore, Hemel Hempstead, Herts

THAT'S INTERESTING...

St Swithun, the Bishop of Winchester was buried out of doors at his own request, but it was decided to move his body to a splendid shrine in the cathedral, and it is said the ceremony was delayed by 40 days' incessant rain.

Colourful climbers
Morning glory

So called because each flower only lasts a day, this beautiful American climber nevertheless produces them continually all summer. There are several pretty varieties to choose from, with flowers in a wide range of colours, and all look wonderful when sunlight shines through their petals. Ipomoeas are only half-hardy so won't survive winter. Sow seeds in March and plant the seedlings outside once all danger of frost has passed. They thrive in sunny well-drained soils and reach 3m in height. Seeds widely available.

Meeting the stars

In 1971, I was PR for the Lord Taverners and this photograph is of Bill Simpson (Dr Finlay) and Bill Crozier (Two Way Family Favourites) at Taverners' cricket match.

Jeannette Simpson, Yelverton, Devon

Bill Crozier and Dr Finlay with his arms round Jeannette

Schooldays remembered

Growing up in South Africa, my schooling started in 1956, my sixth year. Our school year started from the end of January through to November, giving us a long break during mid summer.

I was apprehensive about going to 'big school', as I was a shy child who'd not been to nursery school. The first day was very intimidating and I remember the feeling of desolation as I watched my mother walk away. The child next to me was sobbing and I followed suit until distracted by our lovely teacher.

Our classroom was in a pre-fabricated building on the ground of the local boys' high school, and I can remember returning after break, hot and sweating, along with 30 other or so pupils, squirming uncomfortably, unable to concentrate on the lessons because of the heat. We must have all steamed gently.

Girls were taught sewing and domestic science and the boys, woodwork and handcraft. We made an

Jennifer in 1956

apron and a petticoat out of lawn cotton, all hand-stitched. I hated sewing and was terribly slow, usually with sweaty hands after running out in the hot sun, and never finished my garments which looked slightly grey and limp when I'd finished.

I caught the bus to and from school. When I was kept behind (frequently) for work not completed, I missed the bus and had to walk. The journey, mostly uphill, took about half an hour. In the summer heat, I would buy a penny ice lolly at the local shop at the bottom of the hill, and try to make it last.

Jennifer Garside, Wirksworth, Derbys

Cookery for you

RAPID LAMB WRAPS

Serves: 2-3

- ◆ 4 New Zealand lamb leg steaks
- ◆ 1 tablespoon lemon juice
- ◆ 1 teaspoon ground cumin
- ◆ Salt and pepper
- ◆ 200 g (7 oz) green salad
- ◆ 8 tortilla wraps
- ◆ Selection of dips, eg soured cream and chives, tomato salsa, hummus or guacamole

1 Preheat grill to medium. Pour the lemon juice over the lamb leg steaks, then rub the ground cumin in and season to taste. Grill for 5-8 minutes turning halfway through, until the lamb is just cooked through.

2 Warm the tortilla wraps. Slice the lamb steaks into thin strips and discard the bone. Wrap in the warm tortilla wraps with a handful of green salad, and top with a spoonful of dip.

Tips: A good alternative to tortilla wraps is toasted pitta breads with houmous and an extra squirt of lemon, or for an Indian twist, warm mini naan breads and serve split and filled with the lamb and a minty yoghurt dip or mango chutney.

Recipe courtesy www.lambrecipes.info

Healthier for longer!

Clear your mind – and try meditating for 10 minutes a few times a week. It could help to reduce your blood pressure and lower your stress levels. Sit somewhere quiet, close your eyes and focus on breathing deeply.

TOP TIP

Keep a reel of cotton in the bathroom as an emergency if you run out of dental floss.

THAT'S INTERESTING...

A yurt is a portable, wood lattice-framed dwelling, covered with felt, used by Nomads in Central Asia.

My Grandparents

My maternal Grandfather, Jack Heap, was the only grandparent I knew. He was a miner all his working life and also owned a smallholding where he bred pigs, chickens and ducks for a well known meat company.

I have fond memories of visiting him and helping with the animals. He showed me how to scrub the pigs with a stiff brush to keep their skin clean, and we used to laugh together as the pigs began to nod off with the sheer ecstasy of the treatment!

I helped him prepare their food, tipping scraps into the wood-fired copper, and he'd say to make sure no bacon rind was put in, telling me, 'pigs don't like eating their relatives'.

Every year, a couple of days before Christmas, he would arrive bringing oven ready chicken, home cured bacon, lard, pork scratchings and eggs.

I always picture him, after

Pamela's Granddad as she best remembers him

a busy day, sitting on a log, just thinking and smoking his old beloved Meershaum pipe.

Pamela Hortin, Glenrothes, Fife

Colourful climbers

Dicentra scandens

An unusual climber with nodding, yellow flowers and deeply divided mid green leaves, this plant thrives in partial shade, where many other plants struggle. Sow seed during March and plant out the seedlings when they're several inches in height. Choose the most vigorous and plant it at the base of a piece of trellis, then let it bring a gloomy corner alive. It enjoys moist, well-drained soil and may reach 1.9m in height. Seeds widely available.

Cookery for you

MANGO AND PASSION FRUIT COCKTAIL

Makes 1

- ◆ 5 ice cubes
- ◆ 30 ml (1 fl oz) Belvoir Passion Fruit & Mango Cordial
- ◆ 30 ml (1 fl oz) gin
- ◆ Sparkling spring water, to top up
- ◆ 3 drops of Angostura Bitters
- ◆ 1 fresh passion fruit (optional)

1 Crush the ice in a food processor and place in a champagne glass.
2 Add the cordial and gin
3 Top the glass with the sparkling water and add the Angostura Bitters.
4 Add the pulp of the passion fruit (for texture) and serve immediately.

Recipe courtesy Belvoir Fruit Farms

Healthier for longer!

Get an MOT – ask your GP to check your blood pressure, cholesterol, weight, fitness levels and lung function – knowing how healthy you are (or aren't) will inspire you to keep living well.

My Grandparents

Jeannette, aged 8

Jeannette's beloved Granddad

I loved him dearly – we all did. What tales Grandfather had to tell; a bare fist fighter (an East End champ, no less), French polishing the tables in 10 Downing Street, the treadmill he'd had to walk when he'd been in trouble as a young man, the vigilante group he joined to hunt for Jack the Ripper.

I was nine when he died and too young to go to the funeral, but an elderly aunt insisted I pay my last respects, and my Mum was too tired to argue.

I entered our darkened front room and saw again his shiny bald head – a skating rink for flies, he said – and when I asked where he'd lost his hair, he'd say, 'the Germans shot it off when I was fighting in France'. There too was his moustache turned yellow at the edges where the froth of his beer used to get trapped. 'I'm saving that for later', he'd say with a nod and a wink.

Who would do the card tricks now he was gone? Who'd take us to the pictures, then go out for a pint halfway through the film and say, 'Wait outside for me when it's over. I'll be in the pub next door, and don't tell your Mum'. We never did.

Jeannette Murdoch, Bearsted, Kent

THAT'S INTERESTING...

Did you know that Antonio Vivaldi wrote 500 concertos? And also that he was accused of 'writing the very same concerto 500 times' because almost every work follows the same fast-slow-fast pattern.

TOP TIP

To clean venetian blinds, put white vinegar and water in a dish and, using an old sock, wipe each slat.
Ann Rowlatt, Deeping St James, Cambs

Schooldays remembered

12-year-old Keith

I went to Mersea Council School on Mersea Island, and what I enjoyed most were our outdoor lessons, collecting grasses and leaves and taking them back to press and name.

As we got older, we had our own garden plot where we grew vegetables (this was the 1940s and the war was on). We had lovely school gardens and playing fields.

My friend 'Clapper' Chapman and I were detailed to look after the pigs, so first thing in the morning and late afternoon we mixed the swill and food. This allowed us to miss assembly and other lessons (which I later regretted).

The pigs became very tame and would let us ride on their backs and hold on to their ears until they threw us off!

Keith Lee, Deal, Kent

Colourful climbers
Canary creeper

Tropaeolum peregrinum is an extraordinary plant with deeply divided palm-shaped leaves and heavily fringed blooms. It looks delightful when allowed to scramble through other nearby plants, flowering all summer long. Although tender, it may survive in sheltered gardens if mulched in autumn. Otherwise, grow it as an annual, sowing seed in March and planting out once the frosts have passed. It thrives in a sunny position and may reach 3.5m in height. Seeds widely available.

Meeting the stars

During the late 1950s my cousin Tessa and I were fans of Joe 'Mr Piano' Henderson. We went to see his shows and got to know him quite well. In 1960 we went on holiday to Scarborough where Joe was appearing with Dickie Valentine.

While we were there, we told him that if he was ever to do a summer season in Bournemouth (near to where we lived) we'd like him to come to tea! And he did.

Everything was ready – Granny Legg was sat on the sofa, Auntie Gertie and Mum were busy in the kitchen, and Tessa and I, two excited teenagers, who couldn't wait for him to arrive.

We all sat down to sandwiches, trifles and cakes, and after tea we went into the garden to take some photographs. Then we saw his show again that night – a day we'll never forget.

Jackie Wright, Poole, Dorset

Jackie and Joe

Hampshire: Jane Austen Country

Rural idyll

Although her name is often linked with Bath, Jane Austen lived in Hampshire for the first and last years of her life. She was born in 1775 in the rectory at Steventon where her father was rector and lived there until she was 25. The house has not survived but there is a bronze plaque in the church dedicated to the village's most famous resident.

Jane spent the last years of her life, from 1809 until her death in 1817, in the village of Chawton, near Alton. Her brother, Edward, lived with his family at Chawton House.

Set in a delightful garden, the red-brick house that Jane shared with her mother and her sister, Cassandra, is now a museum containing a collection of her letters and many fascinating family mementoes – including the author's old donkey carriage. On display is the small round table in the parlour where she wrote her best known works; Pride and Prejudice, Emma and Mansfield Park.

As a young girl, Jane often attended dances at neighbouring country houses. One of these, The Vyne, is now owned by the National Trust and is famous for its grand staircase and attractive grounds.

No visit to Hampshire would be complete without seeing the city of Winchester and its ancient cathedral where Jane Austen is buried. In addition to many independent shops, the town has become known for its farmers' market as well as its museums of military history.

Other attractions in Hampshire include walking or riding in the New Forest, now a National Park. Lovers of steam trains won't want to miss a ride on the Watercress Line that runs between Alresford and Alton, while Marwell Zoological Park promises a fine day out for people of all ages.

Ah! Happy Days

It's show time!

Mike Silkstone of Whitby recalls the village show as the highlight of the year

Lots of mining villages held an annual show and ours included horse-riding events and sheepdog trials as well as the all-important horticulture side.

As a social occasion it eclipsed all others. In readiness for the big day, houses and gardens were spruced up, outside privies scrubbed and whitewashed and Mum spent all the previous day baking.

Garden produce was treated with secret recipes handed down from past prize winners. Greenhouse tomatoes were fed with 'tank' (made from sheep droppings, among other things) while outdoor chrysanthemums wore paper bags to stop the rain spoiling their curled petals.

Classes in the show included 'One Rose as Grown', 'Three Pom-Pom, Decorative or Cactus Dahlias' and so on. A children's section entitled us to free entry on a competitor's ticket, provided we turned up with a bunch of wild flowers in a jam jar.

At 11.30 am the tents were cleared for judging but up until the last minute exhibitors would rearranging their entries.

In the afternoon, the marquees opened again and the red, blue and yellow prize tickets propped up against the winning entries. Outside, the show jumping was in progress and the local band was playing marches.

Friends and relatives were invited 'back to our house for tea'. This was a slap up affair. There was a piece of brisket as well as one of our own chickens.

After tea, we'd usually go back to the show field where we'd walk near the turnstile, heads bowed, in the hope that someone had dropped some loose change.

Famous One Liners

PIC: REX FEATURES

Can you match these memorable movie one liners to the films they came from? If you get stuck the answers are below.

1.	"I think this is the beginning of a beautiful friendship."	**A.**	To Have and Have Not
2.	"Don't let's ask for the moon. We have the stars."	**B.**	Titanic
3.	"Every time a bell rings, an angel gets his wings."	**C.**	The Terminator
4.	"I'll be back!"	**D.**	Star Wars
5.	"You know how to whistle, don't you, Steve? You just put your lips together – and blow."	**E.**	Roman Holiday
6.	"I'm the king of the world!"	**F.**	Now, Voyager
7.	"Surely you can't be serious." "I am serious, and don't call me Shirley."	**G.**	North by Northwest
8.	"You came in that thing? You're braver than I thought."	**H.**	It's a Wonderful Life
9.	"Good. For a moment there, I thought we were in trouble."	**I.**	High Society
10.	"Houston - we have a problem."	**J.**	Harvey
11.	"I've never been alone with a man before – even with my dress on."	**K.**	Charade
12.	"You gentlemen aren't REALLY trying to kill my son, are you?"	**L.**	Casablanca
13.	"Well, I've wrestled with reality for 35 years, Doctor, and I'm happy to state I finally won out over it."	**M.**	Butch Cassidy and the Sundance Kid
14.	"End of song, beginning of story."	**N.**	Apollo 13
15.	"How about making me vice president in charge of cheering you up?"	**O.**	Airplane

Answers: 1L, 2F, 3H, 4C, 5A, 6B, 7O, 8D, 9M, 10N, 11E, 12G, 13J, 14I, 15K

A pinch of spice

BY: ROSEMARY FISHER

Beth's cooking will surely lure her errant husband back home...

"I wish you'd told me before I started making this pie," said Beth as she trimmed pastry from the edge of the dish. "It's far too much for me to eat on my own."

"Is that all you've got to say?" asked Alan. "I announce I'm leaving you for another woman and all you're worried about is the size of that pie?"

Beth shrugged: "Never mind. I'll give Dad a ring. Invite him round to dinner. He's always liked steak and kidney pie."

"I can't believe you!"

"Well, I was already aware you've been seeing Dallas Dawkins. I've been told her real name's Dilys, by the way. Not quite so glamorous that, is it?'

"You know her?'

"Who doesn't? Not to speak to, mind. She wouldn't lower herself to talk to someone who actually leaves the house wearing no make-up. I'm not her type at all. Seems you are, though."

Beth often saw Dallas, sashaying around town in revealing tops and tight skirts, her improbably auburn hair kept in place by enough lacquer to destroy a large chunk of the ozone layer.

Beth put the pie in the oven and turned to Alan with a smile. "Off you go, then. Don't let me delay you. I'll see to the steak and kidney while you look after the mutton."

"Mutton? What are you talking about?"

"Think about it," she replied sweetly.

Shaking his head in disbelief, Alan picked up his suitcase. "Do keep in touch," Beth urged politely, opening the front door for him.

After he'd left, she wished she'd made a fuss. Wrapped her arms around him and pleaded with him to stay. But she was more angry than upset. How could Alan have

Women like Dallas ate men like him for breakfast

been taken in by all that false glamour? Yet, he wasn't the first and certainly wouldn't be the last. Women like Dallas ate men like him for breakfast.

Even so, as she lay alone in bed that night, Beth wondered if she should have made more effort with her appearance. Trouble was, she would always rather spend her time cooking, gardening or just curling up with a good book than going to the beauty salon for nail extensions and a fake tan.

It was impossible to imagine Dallas rustling up a plate of home-baked scones or checking her hostas for slugs. But then, Beth thought resentfully as she turned the light off, Dallas was more likely to use a trowel for applying her make-up than weeding her flowerbeds.

Four days later, Alan was back on the doorstep, looking very sheepish.

"Come on in," said Beth. "I'll make a pot of tea and you can tell me all about your little adventure."

"There was no adventure, Beth," he said. "Nothing happened, I promise. It was all over before it even started. We had to go out for dinner every night because Dallas can't cook. Any kind of work is beneath her. If she can't get someone to pay for her meal, she'll get a take-away."

"So that's it," said Beth, producing the pot of tea and a freshly made ginger cake. "You've come home because you're starving."

"No, no, it's not that," Alan protested. "I found out someone had told Dallas I was the manager of Fitzmarks department store. That's why she set her sights on me. As soon as she realised I was only a salesman in electrical goods, she went right off the boil."

"So why has it taken you four whole days to come back?"

"I suppose I can't blame you after what I did. But you didn't waste much time"

ILLUSTRATION: KATE DAVIES

"Ashamed to face you, I suppose. I can't believe I've been so stupid. I don't deserve you."

The phone rang and as she answered it, Beth suggested: "Why don't you go into the garden a minute while I take this call? There's something out there I'd really like you to see."

When she put the receiver down, Alan was standing beside her, his face ashen.

"Well, what do you think?" she asked him. "It's something I've always yearned for so when you

went off with the dreaded Dallas I thought to myself, 'Why not?'"

Alan's look of gloom deepened: "I suppose I can't blame you after what I did. But you didn't waste much time, did you, Beth? And he's so young!"

"Who is?" she said, puzzled.

"That toy boy lounging in our garden! Wasn't that why you sent me out there?'

"What?" Beth rushed outside. Her friend's son, Jason, was sitting on the new recliner, grinning at her.

"Sorry, Beth," he said, "It looked so comfortable I couldn't

resist trying it out and must have fallen asleep."

"Well, thanks for setting the recliner up for me, anyway. And thank your mum for letting me borrow you."

"So it was the recliner you wanted to show me," said Alan, after Jason had left. "You had me seriously worried!"

"Let's go indoors and have that cup of tea," said Beth, linking her arm through his.

"And the ginger cake?"

"Of course. I guessed you'd be back soon so I made it especially. I know it's your favourite."

"Am I forgiven then?" he asked.

"Of course. We all need a little spice in our lives sometimes, don't we?"

Beth smiled to herself as Alan prepared to take a bite of cake. He wasn't to know that she'd mixed in a large spoonful of curry powder instead of ginger.

August 2009

Saturday
1

Sunday
2

Monday
3
Summer Bank Holiday (Scotland)

Tuesday
4

Wednesday
5

Thursday
6

Friday
7
Edinburgh Military tattoo begins

Saturday
8

Sunday
9

Monday
10

Tuesday
11

Wednesday
12

Thursday
13

Friday
14

Saturday
15

Sunday
16

Monday
17

Tuesday
18

Wednesday
19

Thursday
20

Friday
21

Saturday
22

Sunday	Friday
23	28
Monday	Saturday
24	29
Tuesday	Sunday
25	30
Wednesday	Monday
26	31
	Summer Bank Holiday (except Scotland)
Thursday	
27	

Behind the Scenes

Rio Lobo, 1970

An interesting photograph of John Wayne considering his next chess move, between takes on the 1970 film, Rio Lobo.

Like many other film stars, including Humphrey Bogart, Marlon Brando and Charles Boyer, Wayne was a keen chess player.

Rio Lobo was the third film in a trilogy directed by Howard Hawks, and starring John Wayne, with variations on the theme of a sheriff defending his town against various outlaws, the other two being Rio Bravo (1959) and El Dorado (1966). In Rio Lobo, Wayne is trying to find out who sold information to the South during the American Civil War.

John Wayne, who started off his career in silent films in the 1920s, was always closely associated with the all-American genres of the Western and the war film, but he gave a thoughtful performance as an Irish-American boxer who returns to the Ireland of his birth, in John Ford's The Quiet Man (1952).

PIC: REX FEATURES

Carole in the early 1950s

Schooldays remembered

I don't remember too much of my very early schooldays due to an accident I had when I was six, but one thing I do remember was the milk!

At milk time we'd go down in the cellar to get our milk, and in the winter it would be frozen, coming up about three or four inches above the top of the bottle. The bottles would then be put on the heater, and then the milk would be warm and fishy – horrible!

Carole Neville, Axminster, Devon

My Grandparents

My Grandfather ran a grocer's shop in the village of Chalvey, near Slough. I was about four years old in 1939, and I would go with my mother to help Grandpa in the shop.

It was small but well stocked – the range of goods all within close proximity to each other – would give today's environmental health officers a fit!

There was bacon and cheese on the marble top and these, along with butter, margarine, sugar, lard, tea, biscuits and sweets were all weighed out loose on the same scales. In front of the counter were sacks of potatoes, carrots, onions and parsnips all caked with mud, the amount of which varied according to how much rain we'd had.

At the back of the shop was a small shed containing the big tank of paraffin which people used for their lamps.

Customers brought their own containers which Grandpa would fill. He'd then return to the shop and proceed to weigh out whatever the customer wanted next. No hand washing facilities then, so Grandpa would wipe his hands on his pinny which was white in the morning but black and greasy by the end of the day.

He served each customer individually and everyone waited patiently for their turn, usually sitting on the sacks of vegetables.

Most of his customers were women and they loved a bit of gossip but Grandpa would never get involved. He called them all Ma'am and even when asked directly if he'd heard the latest bit of scandal, he would always reply, 'Can't say as I have, Ma'am'.

This picture of Grandpa outside his shop was taken in about 1894. My Grandmother is holding the baby who is my father.

Muriel Aird, Weymouth, Dorset

Cookery for you

HOT AND SOUR CHICKEN AND EXOTIC MUSHROOM SOUP

Serves 4

- ◆ 1 tablespoon groundnut oil
- ◆ 350 g (12 oz) chicken breast fillets, sliced
- ◆ 2.5 cm (1in) fresh root ginger, peeled and grated
- ◆ 1 clove garlic, crushed
- ◆ 1 red chilli, finely chopped
- ◆ 110 g (4 oz) shredded Chinese leaf
- ◆ 150 g (5 oz) exotic mushrooms (eg, oyster, shiitake)
- ◆ 150 g (5 oz) sliced chestnut mushrooms
- ◆ 200 g (7 oz) bamboo shoots, finely sliced
- ◆ 750 ml (1¼ pint) hot vegetable stock
- ◆ 2 tablespoons each dry sherry and light soy sauce
- ◆ 1 tablespoon rice vinegar
- ◆ 3 tablespoons cornflour, mixed with 4 tablespoons cold water
- ◆ 1 spring onion, sliced
- ◆ 1 small handful of coriander, roughly chopped
- ◆ Lime wedges, to serve

1 Heat the oil in a large wok or pan. Add chicken and stir-fry for 4-5 minutes, until pale golden. Add the ginger, garlic and chilli and stir-fry for 10 seconds.
2 Add the Chinese leaf and mushrooms. Stir-fry for 1 min.
3 Then add the bamboo shoots, stock, sherry, soy, vinegar and cornflour mixture. Bring to the boil. Simmer for 1 min.
4 Serve immediately garnished with spring onion, coriander and lime wedges.

Recipe courtesy www.mushroom-uk.com

Colourful climbers
Jasminum officinale

One of the best climbers for scent is jasmine. When in full flower, the scent from this beautiful late summer climber is intoxicating. Train it with wires along a wall near a bedroom window so you can enjoy the scent on a summer's evening. It thrives in full sun and does best in a sheltered position, but is quite vigorous reaching 10m in height, so give it room to spread. Plant widely available.

TOP TIP

If you're on a water meter and you like nice cold drinking water, don't run the tap for ages, just keep a jug of water in the fridge.

Healthier for longer!

Work your core – strengthening your core muscles – the ones under your tummy could help to improve your balance, prevent falls and ease back pain. Pilates is a great way to learn how to do it. Find a class in your area at www.bodycontrol.co.uk

THAT'S INTERESTING…

Hancock's Half Hour was first broadcast on BBC radio, on November 2, 1954. It ran for 101 radio episodes and 59 television episodes.

Cookery for you

BLACK FOREST MERINGUE PIE

Serves 6

Chocolate crumb crust
- ◆ 200 g (7 oz) plain chocolate digestive biscuits
- ◆ 55g (2 oz) butter, melted

Filling
- ◆ 397 g (13 oz) can Carnation Chocolate
- ◆ 110 g (4 oz) ready-to-eat berry fruit mix
- ◆ 2 large egg whites
- ◆ 110g (4 oz) caster sugar, plus extra for sprinkling

1 To make the crust, place biscuits into a food processor and blend to fine crumbs. Tip into a bowl. Add the butter and mix well using a fork. Spoon into a 20 cm (8 in) loose-bottomed fluted tart tin. Press in using the back of a teaspoon.

2 Put the Carnation Chocolate filling into a bowl and stir in the ready-to-eat berry mix. Spoon into the lined case and spread flat. Chill while making the meringue.

3 Preheat the oven to 200°C/400°F/Gas Mark 6. Put the egg whites into a bowl and whisk until stiff. Whisk in the sugar a little at a time to make a thick glossy meringue. Spread over the chocolate tart, making soft peaks.

4 Sprinkle a little caster sugar over the top. Place in the oven for 1–3 minutes until just golden brown.

Recipe courtesy Nestle Carnation, www.carnation.co.uk

Colourful climbers
Mina lobata

An exotic-looking tender perennial, this climber produces flowers that range in colour from scarlet through orange and yellow, to ivory and white. With twining stems, it loves scrambling across trellis, pergolas and archways, reaching 1.7m in height. Sow seed during March and plant out after the frosts have passed, choosing a sunny sheltered site with a moist well-drained soil and provide them with something to climb. Seeds widely available.

My Grandparents

Joan's Grandparents

My grandparents came to the country from London to Braughing in Hertfordshire. I used to stay with them and they would take me on trips to the seaside.

They kept a pig down the garden and Gran used to feed it and rub it with cream when it was hot. Happy memories.   **Joan M Barker, Ware, Herts**

Schooldays remembered

Smile please! Ann is in the second row, in the middle

I went to Percy Street Infants' School, Old Basford, Nottingham, an old Victorian building, now demolished.

I enjoyed music and singing, and on one occasion I played Snow White, probably because I was the tallest in the class (now I'm only 5ft 2).

At Guildford Secondary School for Girls, I was in the school choir, and we performed at Nottingham's Albert Hall in a competition, and came 13th out of 50.

I enjoyed history, which was one of my best subjects, and I now love delving into family history, which is fascinating.

**Ann Rowlatt,
Deeping St James, Cambs**

THAT'S INTERESTING...

In August 1930 Clarence Birdseye patented a method for packaging frozen foods.

TOP TIP

Pack a reel of sticky tape when you go on holiday – great for all sorts of emergencies, such as sealing leaking toiletry bottles.

Healthier for longer!

Go for a mammogram – not only could it pick up potential breast cancer it could also highlight your stroke risk. Women with calcifications on their mammograms have a higher risk of stroke. The earlier you discover your risks the more time you have to make life saving changes.

Meeting the stars

My dear friend Nora emigrated to America in 1953, settling in New York. On one of my visits to her, she asked if I would like to meet a great lady – actress Gloria Swanson? Nora had been a manageress in a health food store, and Gloria asked to be served by 'that nice English girl'. Their friendship grew through their mutual interests in painting, sculpting and yoga.

I was nervous when I realised I was going to meet a world famous film star in her home. Nora and I both wore hats and rang the bell of her apartment. We were greeted by a dark suited butler wearing white gloves.

We walked across a spacious hallway to another door, where another butler rang the bell. The door opened, and there was Gloria in a full-length pink dress. She asked us into a large lounge full of interesting items, a

Jean's friend Nora with Gloria, in Tennessee

world globe, a huge painting of a granddaughter, a sculpture of a pair of hands.

We sat at a long coffee table for apple juice and biscuits, and I remember her beautiful blue eyes and lovely teeth fascinated me.

My last vivid memory of her was of her standing in the inner doorway, waving goodbye. I was so pleased my friend had given me the chance to meet Gloria.

**Jean Artist,
Bradford, W Yorks**

Cookery for you

BROCCOLI AND BACON QUICHE

Serves 4

Colourful climbers
Sweet pea

Everyone loves sweet peas and, as hardy annuals, they're remarkably easy to grow. Although there are hundreds of varieties to choose between, one of the prettiest is 'Matucana'. One of the first to be introduced into Britain before 1700 by a Sicilian monk Franciscus Cupani, it has deep blue flowers with purple wings and a captivating scent. Sow seeds in spring or autumn and plant out when large enough to handle. Seeds widely available.

- ◆ 500 g (1 lb 2 oz) shortcrust pastry
- ◆ 1 tablespoon olive oil
- ◆ 110 g (4 oz) bacon *lardons
- ◆ 1 garlic clove finely chopped
- ◆ 350 g (12 oz) broccoli
- ◆ 4 free range eggs
- ◆ 200 ml (7 fl oz) double cream
- ◆ Salt and cracked black pepper

* Small pieces of thick cut bacon, sold ready-chopped

1. Preheat the oven to 200°C/400°F/Gas Mark 6
2. Roll out the pastry and use it to line a 16cm (6½ inch) springform tin. Prick the base of the pastry and chill.
3. Heat the oil in a small frying pan, add the lardons and cook until almost crisp. Add the garlic and cook for 30 seconds. Remove from the heat and leave to cool slightly, then sprinkle over the pastry base. Fill the case with broccoli.
5. Beat the eggs and cream, and season. Pour into the case.
6. Bake for 45 minutes or until set. Serve warm with a green salad.

Recipe courtesy Tenderstem® broccoli, www.tenderstem.co.uk

Healthier for longer!

Eat more omega-3s – as well as keeping your heart healthy they could help to protect your brain from Parkinson's disease. Get your quota from oily fish such as salmon and mackerel and nuts and seeds such as almonds and linseeds.

THAT'S INTERESTING...

Cuckoo, cuckoo, what do you do?
In April I open my bill
In May I sing both night and noon
In June I change my tune
In July away I fly
In August away I must

Three generations: Mavis's Grandma, her mother and her son

My Grandparents

I only knew one Grandparent, my maternal Granma. My Gran helped my mother to bring up her five children, often being there when they were born.

Gran was always busy, knitting for us all, making rag rugs, doing the vegetables for our meals and often making pease pudding to fill us up.

Gran had very long hair which she would put up into a bun with dozens of hair pins which we would often find on the floor.

At times she'd go and stay with her other daughters for a while, but we were always pleased to have her back with us, as I suppose she spoiled us a little!

Mavis Mansfield, Worthing, Sussex

Schooldays remembered

I still remember my first day at school which was at Priory Road, High Wycombe in 1957, aged four. I had no idea where mum was taking me or what I would be doing when she walked off and left me… I cried inconsolably. Not going for half a day and building up slowly, it was 8.55am to 3.50pm, and I didn't like it.

I was a fat child with a funny surname (Strange), and a bit slow to learn, and as a result I was teased, bullied and blamed for things I hadn't done. By spending playtimes and lunch in hiding, I managed to avoid getting into trouble but it affected my ability to make friends and meant that sometimes I'd be hungry because I hadn't had my school dinner.

However, as the years progressed, things got better; my schoolwork improved and I became a dinner girl in the staffroom.

When I was 11, I changed schools. I'd always been good at English but not so good at maths, and so I failed my prelim exam which meant I didn't get to take the 11+, much to my parents' dismay.

So I went to Hatters Lane Secondary School, which I left in 1969, starting then in an office, having done shorthand and typing at school. I would have liked to have stayed on in the newly-created sixth form and take A levels but my dad had the old view that it was my duty to leave school and start contributing towards the household, and not even my headmistress could change his mind.

Judith Brown, Hereford

Above: Judith with her mum in 1955
Left: 14-year-old Judith in 1967

Cookery for you

WATERCRESS, BANANA & KIWI SMOOTHIE

Serves 2

◆ 85g (3½ oz) watercress
◆ 1 medium banana, roughly chopped
◆ 1 kiwi fruit, peeled and chopped
◆ 275 ml (½ pint) pomegranate or cranberry juice

1 Place the watercress in a food processor or liquidiser and blend until finely chopped.
2 Add the banana and kiwi fruit. Blend again until smooth. With the motor running, gradually pour in the juice and blend until smooth. Serve immediately.

Recipe courtesy The Watercress Alliance

▮ THAT'S INTERESTING...

In severe heat a camel can survive four to seven days without drinking, but it can go 10 months without drinking at all if it is not working and the forage contains enough moisture.

▮ TOP TIP

Can't find the corkscrew? Don't panic! Screw a metal hook into the cork, put a wooden spoon handle through the hook and pull the cork out.

My Grandparents

Dorothea's grandparents in Bray, 1932

My Gran worked at a milliner's before she was married in 1891. One day, when making a hat, she gave the brim a different twist but was unable to get it back into the standard shape. She just had to leave it and hoped it wouldn't be noticed.

Later on that day she was sent for and, in her words, 'Went to the owner's room in fear and trembling'. But instead of receiving a sharp reprimand, she was told to make a dozen more hats with the same twist to the brim as a well-respected customer had been in and bought the original, saying how attractive it was!

Dorothea Abbott, Stratford-upon-Avon, Warks

Healthier for longer!

Stay upbeat – it could protect your bones. Scientists have discovered a link between depression and osteoporosis in post menopausal women. This could be because depressed people are less likely to exercise, eat well and spend time in bone boosting sunshine.

Schooldays remembered

Irene in her school photograph

I started school around 1957, and during lessons we sat round a table, in the middle of which was the cardboard 'Tidy box' in which we kept our pencils and crayons. Sometimes we played with clay on our little boards – I can still feel the clammy coldness – or played in the sand tray.

My first Christmas I made a spill-holder complete with paper spills for my Dad to light his pipe with, but I went down with measles and Miss Ashurst delivered it to our house. I can remember my family crowding to the door to see 'our Irene's teacher' as she walked away.

The milk monitor at our school removed the foil top with a little gadget shaped like a flying saucer. And we could buy 'cheesettes' from the biscuit monitor – I would buy 24 and wolf the lot (happy days – I only have to walk past a cheesette now and I put on 2lbs).

Someone might bring a sheet of 'transfers' to school, with pictures of maybe a Union Jack, a doll or a boat. We stuck them face down on our arms by licking the backing paper, which we carefully peeled off after a few minutes, leaving a 'tattoo' behind.

Irene Roberts, Wigan, Lancs

Colourful climbers
Allamanda

A native of Brazil, Allamanda cathartica may be tender but will flower several months of the year in a sunny conservatory. Evergreen with large, yellow, trumpet-shaped blooms. it's one of the showiest plants in the tropical collection at St Andrews Botanic garden, so is worth growing at home, if you have the room. Take care, though, as it can be quite rampant reaching several metres in height.

Meeting the stars

I met Ronald Reagan in 1949 – long before he was President but when he was a movie star.

My friend's parents were separated, and the only way she could see her father, Len, who was a doorman at London's Savoy Hotel, was to visit him at work. One morning Len told us Ronald Reagan was staying there, and I asked him if could try

and get his autograph for me.

Ronald was in England promoting his new film, The Hasty Heart, with Patricia Neal and Richard Todd, and Len told us to tuck ourselves in a corner, so we could get a quick look at him when the car came to pick him up.

We saw Len approach Ronald and open the door for him – then they looked in our direction and came towards us. That giant smile and a 'Hello girls, I'm running late but I'll get a signed photo to you. It was very nice of you to wait to see me'. Bliss! That was the first time I heard the expression, 'Have a nice day'. Sadly, the photograph, 'To Hilda, much love Ronald Reagan' was thrown away without my knowledge.

Hilda Gallagher, Romford, Essex

PIC: REX FEATURES

Writers' Britain

Lincoln: Tennyson Country

Wolds and Fens

Alfred, Lord Tennyson was born August 6, 1809 at the rectory in the Lincolnshire village of Somersby where his father was the rector. The handsome Georgian house is now privately owned but a bust of the poet can be seen in the church of St Mary's.

The village is in the rolling countryside of the Lincolnshire Wolds and the stream at its west end is said to have been the inspiration for Tennyson's poem, The Brook. The unspoilt Wolds are popular with walkers and cyclists.

Tennyson was one of 12 children and the whole family went for their holidays to the East coast resorts of Skegness and Mablethorpe. The house that they rented in Mablethorpe still stands; it is called Tennyson's Cottage and can be found on the coast road to the north of the town centre.

Now owned by The National Trust, Gunby Hall in Spilsby was familiar to the poet as a young man. He described it as 'an English home…all things in order stored, a haunt of peace' and this quotation in his handwriting has been framed and hung on the wall in the library.

Tennyson scholars head to the city of Lincoln where the Tennyson Research Centre is housed in the dome of Lincoln Central Library which also has an exhibition that includes the poet laureate's hat and cloak among other items.

Other attractions in this fine old city are its Norman castle, which offers magnificent views across the surrounding area as far as the Fens, and the ancient cathedral with its distinctive three towers. An imposing statue of Tennyson by G F Watts stands in the cathedral grounds.

Down Rainbow Hill

Ah! Happy days

For Estella Thomson of Worcester the allotments were her adventure playground

Estella and her mother on the 'lotties'

Whenever I smell sweet peas, I think of 'nuncle' Harry. He was not my real uncle but a neighbour who lived in the council house adjoining ours. I loved our address – Green Lane, Rainbow Hill.

My mother had to go out to work so uncle collected me from school on the days when he had an early shift on the railway. He would be waiting at the school gates with his wheelbarrow and used to lift me up like a queen on a throne of pig nuts or 'hoss muck' from which I was protected by sheets of The Daily Mirror.

Then we set off to the allotments – or 'the lotties', as we called them. Our first job was to see to the pig. Nuncle made me stand back while he lit the fire under the copper and put the scraps on to cook. These were mixed with pig nuts and fed to the pig who slurped them noisily.

I remember sitting on the wooden bench, fat little legs dangling, eating bread and rosemary lard, swilled down with 'corporation pop' (tap water).

My first exercise in writing was scratching my initials, MAB, on the side of a marrow and watching them grow larger every week. Nuncle told me that Mab was the name of the queen of the fairies.

These days, planting my sweet pea seeds always brings back memories of Nuncle. And I remember his words: "Seeds hold the promise of heavenly perfume and butterfly flowers."

Summers on the beach

Ann Rowe remembers her childhood days in Broadstairs

'All I want for Christmas is My Two Front Teeth...' sings Ann

I n 1951 my family moved to Broadstairs, Kent from Manchester because us three children had all been sickly and the doctor said we needed 'the air on the South Coast'. I was 18 months old, my brother Robert, four-and-a-half, and my sister Helen a year older.

My parents bought a boarding house in St Mary's Road but my father found a job as a telephonist at the House of Commons in London and only came home at weekends.

He'd arrive home on a Friday night, always with a treat for us. Once it was a stuffed toy dog each, complete with different colour collars so that we could tell them apart. Another time it was a tin of mandarin orange segments – we'd never seen these before, and such anticipation as it was opened!

I wonder now how my mother coped. During the summer months we moved up to the attic rooms so that all the bedrooms on the lower floors could be let to holidaymakers. Each morning my mother carried jugs of hot water to each room for the holidaymakers to wash. She'd then cook a full breakfast for them, and in the evening a cooked 'tea' .

With mum always busy and dad away, the three of us had a lot of freedom, and we'd sit playing on the beach until dark. There was a weekly children's talent show at the Bandstand and you'd nearly always see me in the line up singing All I want for Christmas is My Two Front Teeth. I didn't have much of a voice but the fact I really didn't have any front teeth ensured applause and laughter, and I usually walked away with a stick of rock!

There was also a café on the beach which was raised up. We'd sit under it sifting through the sand for any money that had fallen through the café floor slats. It kept us in ice creams and sweets throughout the summer!

Sometimes I'd put my teddies and dolls in a basket and take them up to Piedmont Park for a picnic.

Although my mother worked hard during the day, she would often take us for long walks in the summer evenings. We regularly walked into Ramsgate where we might share a bag of chips and a ride on the miniature railway.

We lived there until I was eight, when we moved to London to be with dad. London was another big adventure but it was soon clear that the freedom we'd enjoyed in Broadstairs was not available to us anymore.

September 2009

Tuesday
1

Wednesday
2

Thursday
3

Friday
4

Saturday
5

Sunday
6

Monday
7

Tuesday
8

Wednesday
9

Thursday
10

Friday
11

Saturday
12

Sunday
13

Monday
14

Tuesday
15

Wednesday
16

Thursday
17

Friday
18

Saturday
19

Sunday
20

Monday
21

Tuesday
22

Wednesday **23**	Sunday **27**
Thursday **24**	Monday **28**
Friday **25**	Tuesday **29**
Saturday **26**	Wednesday **30**

Behind the Scenes

The Sound of Music, 1965

Lessons must go on, even if you're appearing in one of the most iconic films of the 20th century – The Sound of Music (1965). It was school, though not quite as most children would know it, for the performers who played the von Trapp children, Liesl (Charmian Carr), Friedrich (Nicholas Hammond), Louisa (Heather Menzies), Kurt (Duane Chase), Brigitta (Angela Cartwright), Marta (Debbie Turner) and Gretl (Kym Karath).

Location scouting in Salzburg had started as early as 1963, and filming began in spring of the following year. The schedule was tight but the only thing that couldn't be planned for was the weather – rain, rain and more rain! So shooting took place in the covered sets when the elements proved too much for cast and crew.

Interesting to note, too, that the real Maria was sent from the convent to the von Trapp family to care for just one of the children, who had scarlet fever, and not as governess to all the children.

Schooldays remembered

I went to our local infants school when I was five in 1932. It was a small building, completely made out of corrugated iron sheets, and known locally as the Tin School.

There were only two classes, housed in one large room, and, after assembly, a deep green curtain would be fixed across the room which divided our two classes. Although we were aware of the lesson being taught on the other side of the curtain it didn't bother us.

The atmosphere was very happy and I don't remember any child playing truant. One teacher's husband was a clever carpenter, and he made us a wonderful dolls' house and a Noah's Ark, complete with wooden animals. If any child was distressed they would be allowed to play with the Ark until they felt better.

Our playground was a small area in front of the school, with a short wooden fence. On special days, such as Empire Day, we all took flags to school and put on a display of marching and singing for our mothers, who would watch us over the fence.

**Christine Widger,
Leicester**

My Grandparents

Sarah and Percy Robertshaw were my grandparents and lived in Girlington, Bradford. In 1954 my brother, Simon, and I went to live with them; they never called one another by their Christian names – Nan was 'Buds' and Granddad, 'Long Legs'.

From spring until autumn Granddad spent most of his days at his allotment and, at weekends, we were never far behind. I'd go into his greenhouse and smell the ripe-red tomatoes. Our job was to weigh the produce into pounds and half pounds and put them in thick off-white greaseproof bags. Then we handed

Nan 'Buds' with Joan at Christmas

the goods to Granddad's customers on the way home; we loved knocking on the door, taking the money and giving it to Granddad.

Granddad was a stylishly attired gentleman away from the allotment – Sunday was his day off, and he dressed in a suit, highly polished boots and trilby hat.

Nan Robertshaw had worked hard all her life. Aged 12 she'd started work part-time; the morning at school and the afternoon working at a milliner's shop. On foot, she delivered hat boxes filled with the latest styles to the wealthy home owners in Manningham, Heaton and surrounding houses.

Living with our grandparents, we were never ignored. We were always included in conversations and asked our opinion. I often wonder what would have happened to my brother and me without Buds and Long Legs.

Joan Davico, Bradford

Granddad 'Long Legs' by his greenhouse

Cookery for you

PESTO CHICKEN AND PASTA SALAD

Serves 4

- ◆ 2 chicken breast fillets
- ◆ 1 teaspoon olive oil
- ◆ 4 tablespoons pine nuts, toasted
- ◆ 150 g (5 oz) pasta shells
- ◆ ½ red onion, sliced
- ◆ 225 g (8 oz) cherry tomatoes, halved
- ◆ 175 g (6 oz) cucumber, deseeded and cut into sticks
- ◆ 120 g (4 ½ oz) Italian salad leaves

For the dressing:
- ◆ 1 tablespoon olive oil
- ◆ 2 tablespoons pesto sauce
- ◆ 1 tablespoon red wine vinegar

1 Preheat a griddle pan. Brush both sides of the chicken with the oil and season well. Cook the chicken breasts on the griddle for 15-20 mins, turning once until golden brown and cooked through. Thinly slice.

2 Meanwhile, boil the pasta for 8-10mins, or until just cooked and still 'al dente'. Drain and run under cold water to cool, then place in a large bowl.

3 Add the chicken, pine nuts, onion, tomatoes and cucumber. Mix the dressing ingredients together and toss into the salad bowl. Season to taste.

4 Add the salad leaves and toss again to mix. Serve immediately.

Recipe courtesy UK Salad Producers

Colourful climbers
Campsis 'Madame Galen

A large, vigorous and exotic climber, 'Madame Galen' is the hardiest variety of this plant, with large clusters of orange-red bell-shaped flowers in late summer and early autumn. It's tender, so grows best on a south-facing wall but may outgrow its space. Prune it hard every year in late winter so the new growth has time to ripen. It thrives in full sun and well-drained soil and may reach 10m in height. Plants widely available.

TOP TIP

Use the measuring balls from washing powder (liquid) as water containers when the grandchildren are painting.

Molly Sampson, Mirfield, W Yorks

Healthier for longer!

Have an argument – it could add years to your life. Although anger and hostility could up your risk of heart disease, keeping your rage bottled up won't help either. US scientists have found that husbands and wives who suppress their anger during a row had a higher risk of early death compared to those who expressed it. So get talking.

THAT'S INTERESTING...

The Great Fire of London began on Sunday, September 2, 1666 and raged for four days. It completely gutted the medieval city of London and more than 13,000 houses went up in smoke.

Cookery for you

BANOFFEE OR FRUIT ICE CREAM POTS

Serves 4

- ◆ 570 ml (1 pint) good quality vanilla ice cream
- ◆ 1 Mars Bar, chopped
- ◆ 100 ml (4 fl oz) double cream
- ◆ 1 medium banana, sliced, or 100 ml (4 fl oz) fruit compote or coulis

1 In a small saucepan, melt the Mars Bar over a low heat. Add the cream and stir to combine and leave to cool.
2 Scoop the ice cream into four dishes.
3 Drizzle over the chocolate sauce and bananas, or fruit compote, as desired.

Recipe courtesy the Britsh Asparagus Growers' Association,

Healthier for longer!

Get fit – your fitness levels are even more important than what the scales say, according to the experts. People over 60 who are fit live longer, regardless of their levels of body fat. If you keep fit you're likely to have a stronger heart and lungs than a less active person.

My Grandparents

My Grandfather Horatio went out to South Africa after fighting in the First World War. There was little work in England and South Africa offered employment; he was a coppersmith and worked on the railways. He arrived in the city of Durban and rented a room in a boarding house, where he met Peggy, whom he later married.

We usually visited the grandparents on Friday evenings and there was always something to do. My Grandfather loved a singsong, and we were encouraged to put on plays and musicals – with much applause for our efforts, although there was little talent among us.

They taught us card games and, best of all, carpet bowls. Most of all, our Grandpa could – and did – stand on his head! We usually joined him and often there would be a row of grandchildren of all sizes, standing on our heads, Grandpa among us.

My mother was astonished that her father, who had been so strict with his own children, was so free and easy with us.

Granny was a tiny lady, just topping 5ft, and I loved her dearly. She was gentle and kind, and I never recall her raising her voice. She was my ally during my difficult teenage years, I always knew that nothing I did would stop her from loving me.

Jennifer Garside, Wirksworth, Derbyshire

Peggy and Horatio Davis

■ THAT'S INTERESTING...

85% of all greetings cards are bought by women!

Schooldays remembered

Helen (second left) with her family

I was a shy girl, a bit of a swot and good at the three Rs. I loved writing in my copybook with pen and ink.

However, I was really pathetic at anything involving running, jumping, catching and throwing. I was always the last person chosen to join a team, even for rounders.

One glance at the gym hall put me off when I saw the dreaded wall bars – just the thought of trying to clamber up them, or trying to vault over the wooden horse… There I stood in my navy knickers wishing the floor would open up and swallow me.

Oh happy days when I left all this behind me to sit at an office desk – with my pen and ink, of course.

Helen Gibb, Penicuik, Midlothian

Meeting the stars

While I was in Ceylon (now Sri Lanka) from 1955 to 1957, in the RAF, I had the chance to work on the film, The Bridge On The River Kwai on location at Kitulgala. We met Sir Alec Guinness, Jack Hawkins and William Holden.

William Holden always had time for a chat, with questions about England, and what we did in the RAF. We took all our annual leave, plus borrowed time to work on the film set and were paid £5 per day.

The cost of building the bridge was $250,000 and took eight months to construct. It was destroyed in seconds with 1,000 tonnes of dynamite, with six separate cameras filming its destruction.

Barry Frow, South Humberside

Barry (left) with William Holden

Colourful climbers
Clematis 'Pagoda'

One of the late-flowering texensis group of clematis, 'Pagoda' flowers in late summer producing pretty, bell-shaped blooms of greyish-pink and purple – a lovely colour combination. It thrives in sun or partial shade and does best in well-drained soil. Prune it back hard in early spring. Plants are available from specialist clematis nurseries such as Caddicks Clematis at www.caddicks-clematis.co.uk

TOP TIP

If possible, shop at your local supermarket half an hour before it closes – there should be lots of items marked down in price.

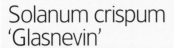

Colourful climbers

Solanum crispum 'Glasnevin'

A relative of the humble potato, Solanum crispum 'Glasnevin' originates in Chile, but grows happily in sheltered gardens in this country. It's semi-evergreen and requires plenty of support but produces attractive lilac flowers during summer and autumn. It enjoys a sunny position and moist but well-drained soil and reaches 1.8m in height. Plants widely available.

Healthier for longer!

Give something back – volunteering could make your retirement happier and longer, according to research by the British Psychological Society. Mentoring other people or working in a charity shop is a great way to keep your mind active too.

THAT'S INTERESTING...

The making of corn dollies was a Pagan custom and evolved among corn-growing people who believed that the spirit of the corn lived in the crop.

SALMON, SHIITAKE AND MIXED MUSHROOM EGG FRIED RICE

Serves 4

- ◆ 175 g (6 oz) Jasmine rice
- ◆ 110 g (4 oz) frozen peas
- ◆ 350 g (12 oz) organic salmon fillets
- ◆ 2 tablespoons groundnut oil
- ◆ 3 eggs, beaten
- ◆ 350 g (12 oz) sliced mixed mushrooms (eg, closed/open cup, Portobello, shiitake)
- ◆ 3 tablespoons soy sauce
- ◆ 1 tablespoon sesame oil
- ◆ Juice of half a lemon

1 Cook the rice for 10 minutes or until tender. Add the peas for the last 2 mins cooking time. Drain and set aside.

2 Place the salmon in a large saucepan, add 6 tablespoons water and bring to the boil. Cover and simmer for 8 minutes, or until the fish is opaque and cooked through. Transfer to a plate, remove any skin and break into flakes. Set aside.

3 Heat a wok over high heat and add half the oil. Add the eggs to the pan and cook, stirring until the egg is scrambled. Transfer to a plate. Wipe out the wok, return it to the heat and when hot, add the remaining oil. Add the mushrooms and stir-fry for 2 minutes. Add the rice, peas, salmon, eggs, soy sauce, sesame oil and lemon juice and gently mix. Once piping hot, serve immediately.

Recipe courtesy www.mushrooms-uk.com

My Grandparents

Sidney and Alice in 1914
Below, left: Alice's pocket watch

My Grandmother Alice was young, pretty and single, and worked in a big house in London as a housemaid. Unfortunately, she caught the eye of the son of a neighbouring house and in 1911 this was frowned upon. He gave her a beautiful decorated pocket watch for her 18th birthday present, but the gift was discovered by the housekeeper.

Alice was summarily packed off to her employer's country house to end the romance and the city girl was destined to spend the rest of her life in rural Berkshire. She never complained about the hard life in the country. Three years later she married my Grandfather Sidney Money, who worked on the estate.

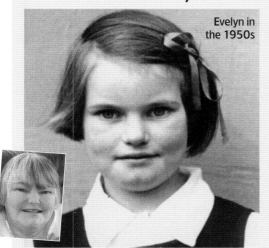

She kept the watch and in later life, told my father how she came by it. After her death my father inherited it and I now have it.

Grandfather Sidney went to fight for his country in 1916, and was sent to the Somme with the 4th Royal Berkshire Regiment. After months of battle, one night as darkness fell, the platoon found a barn and were told they could rest there for the night.

My Grandfather saw a pile of hay at the far end of the barn and, although exhausted, managed the extra walk. Just as he reached the hay, a German shell hit the other end of the barn, killing the rest of the platoon and badly wounding my Grandfather, but he survived.

Sidney and Alice were very happy but would she have had such a happy life if she'd been allowed to continue her romance with the London youth

Wendy J Wearing, Begbroke, Oxon

Schooldays remembered

Evelyn in the 1950s

Infant school memories… Walking three miles to school at four-and-a-half in 1951, black metal coat pegs. Moving into the juniors… poetry was a favourite subject for when Miss Weetman called out a name, silence reigned, 'A wet sheet and a flowing sea, And a wind that follows fast'.

Knitting dishcloths: I spent more hours standing by the desk waiting for a dropped stitch to be picked up – why did my finished cloth still have ladders?

Lunch time and squares of oilcloth on the desks, to put sandwiches on, and 3d for a cup of cocoa. No hot food or canteens, although by 1957 we had plastic plates, the white one for the headmistress, the colours for the pupils.

Evelyn Jones, Shrewsbury, Shrops

Cookery for you

MACADAMIA SHORTCAKE SLICE

Makes 24

- ◆ 250 g (9 oz) butter, softened to room temperature
- ◆ 175 g (6 oz) fine caster sugar, plus 1 tablespoon extra
- ◆ 4 eggs
- ◆ 225 g (8 oz) self-raising flour, sifted
- ◆ 110 g (4 oz) macadamia halves
- ◆ 6 tablespoons warmed apricot conserve

1 Preheat oven to 180°C/350°F/Gas Mark 4. Grease a 30 x 20 x 4cm (12 x 8 x 1½ inch) deep pan and line base with baking paper.
2 Beat the butter and sugar together in a bowl until thick and creamy. Beat in the eggs one at a time.
3 Stir in the flour and half the nuts to make a fairly stiff mixture.
4 Using a spatula, spread half the mixture over the pan base. Then spoon over the warm conserve.
5 Spread the remaining cake mixture over to reach pan sides. Press in the remaining macadamias and sprinkle with caster sugar.
6 Bake for 25-30 minutes, or until a skewer inserted comes out clean. If the macadamia nuts brown too much, cover with baking paper.
7 Remove from heat and stand for 5 minutes before turning out onto a rack to cool. Cut into squares.

Recipe courtesy Macadamia Advice Centre, www.Macadamias.org.uk

My Grandparents

Sheila's Granny and Granddad

My mother's father was a farmer in Wickenby, near Lincoln, and I used to love threshing days in late September when the men came with their machines – we used to get filthy in the process!

The long wooden kitchen table was set up for the men's dinners; my grandmother and mother had cooked steak and kidney puddings in large basins tied up with cloth and steamed for what seemed like hours, and made pans of steaming broth, with rice pudding for afters. Us kids had watched the men at work all morning, then we'd eat the leftovers!

Later when I was about 11 years old, the farm was sold on, and I remember my uncle who had always lived at home, running up and down with the horses for sale, and the farm implements set out in the field. My grandparents then moved to a thatched cottage in the village.

The picture of Granny and Granddad was taken the year I was born (1932), on the wedding day of their eldest granddaughter.

Sheila Wood, Lincoln

TOP TIP

For a makeshift kneeling mat when gardening, old sheets of bubble wrap are ideal.
Molly Sampson, Mirfield, W Yorks

THAT'S INTERESTING...

The first commercial shown on British TV in Britain was for Gibbs SR toothpaste and was transmitted on the evening of Sept 22, 1955 during a show hosted by Jack Jackson.

Schooldays remembered

Myra (middle, second row) in Class 2

How we ever learned anything at school during the war is difficult to imagine, (although most of us left school numerate and literate) because we seemed to spend so much time in the air raid shelter where we sang, knitted squares to clean our slates or just talked.

At other times, we practised diving under our desks in case we didn't have time to get to the shelter. And we were taught to fall flat on the ground in case we were out in the street, to save us from the blast and flying debris.

From time to time, a fireman (I think it was) came to the school to check our gas masks, to make sure the rubber hadn't perished. My father also used to check mine and, to my dismay, stuck red bicycle patches over any pinholes he found. The tears I shed over those patches; I thought I'd be told off for how they looked. But the man said, "My, you have a good Dad who must love you, the way he's protected you with those patches!"

Myra Barklem, London E4

Healthier for longer!

Go brown – when it comes to rice that is. It's packed with magnesium, which along with calcium is essential for strong, healthy bones. Brown rice not your thing? Spinach and other green vegetables are also crammed with it.

Colourful climbers
C aromatica

Few clematis are scented but C aromatica makes up for this omission by producing superbly fragrant blooms between July and September. A graceful climber, its elegant creamy stamens contrast wonderfully with the blue-tinted violet sepals. It's a non-clinging variety so does best if planted in a basket or container, or allowed to scramble across the ground. Plants are available from specialist clematis nurseries such as Caddicks Clematis at www.caddicks-clematis.co.uk

Meeting the stars

I was living in Cardiff and a journalist friend of mine asked me if I would like to meet Cliff. We went to interview him between the first and second shows at the Gaumont Theatre. This was in 1961, when Cliff and I were both 20. He was very nice and I remember he had holes in his socks!

Pauline Jefford, Sandbach, Cheshire

Cliff and Pauline

The Lake District: Beatrix Potter Country

Fairytale fells

PIC WWW.CUMBRIAPHOTO.CO.UK

A London girl, Beatrix Potter first went to the Lake District in 1882 when she was 16 and her family spent a holiday at Wray Castle near Ambleside. While there, she made friends with the vicar of Wray church, Cannon H Rawnsley, and it was he who later encouraged her to publish her first book, The Tale of Peter Rabbit.

In 1905, she used the earnings from her books to buy Hill Top farm near Sawtrey which provided her with a retreat from life in the city. Her next purchase was nearby Castle Cottage to which she moved in 1913 following her marriage to a local solicitor,

William Heelis. The couple lived there for 30 years.

William Heelis's office in Hawkshead is now home to the National Trust's Beatrix Potter Gallery which contains many of her original sketchbooks, watercolours and manuscripts. The delightful town is the setting for her book The Tale of Johnny Town Mouse.

Tarn Hows, a mile outside Hawkshead, is part of the 4,000 acres of property that Beatrix Potter bequeathed to The National Trust. A walk around the tarn takes about an hour and is suitable for wheelchairs.

Fans of Jemima Puddleduck

and Mrs Tiggywinkle should also visit The World of Beatrix Potter attraction at Bowness-on-Windermere where they can see recreations of their favourite characters followed by tea in the Tailor of Gloucester Tea Rooms.

For the less active, an excursion to Levens Hall and its remarkable topiary garden, first laid out in 1694, provides a pleasant day out.

Another Eliza Doolittle

Ah! Happy days

Being an evacuee was a culture shock for Mrs Jean Darby of Swaffham, Norfolk

I grew up in Lambeth in the east end of London where I lived in Randall Row Buildings with my father, grandmother, uncle and two aunts. My mother had died of TB when I was two.

We lived in a basement flat with three rooms but no bathroom. We used to go to the public baths which were hot and steamy. Each cubicle had a bath and a chair for our clothes. I would sit outside while Nan bathed and then she bathed me. I still remember how cold the stone floor was.

Every day at school we were given a small bottle of milk and a spoonful of malt. On May 1 every year we danced around a maypole put up in the playground. We all held a ribbon tied to the top of the pole and we ducked under and over each other as we danced around it to make a pretty pattern of coloured ribbons.

After school, we played hopscotch in the street,

or waited outside the pub, drinking pop and eating arrowroot biscuits.

After war broke out, I was evacuated to Exmouth in Devon where I was chosen by a couple who told me to call them Uncle Brian and Aunt Dorothy. They lived in a large, three-storey house with three bathrooms and three kitchens. Uncle Brian was a very important person on the Council.

My cockney accent irritated Aunt Dorothy so she gave me elocution lessons. I had to recite: 'Hit him on the head with a huge heavy hammer and make him holler until he is hoarse'. I used to meet my friend Eileen on the beach after school and we'd fall about laughing over this.

When I went back to London during the school holidays my nan and aunts were angry with me because I kept correcting their speech. I couldn't win.

I now pronounce you...

Romance is in the air! Simply match the star to their famous partner. If you get stuck the answers are at the bottom of the page.

PIC: REX FEATURES

Right: Spencer Tracy gave Elizabeth Taylor away in the classic movie, 'The Father of the Bride' but who did she marry in real life?

1.	John Alderton	A.	Ali MacGraw
2.	Desi Arnaz	B.	Annette Bening
3.	Humphrey Bogart	C.	Ava Gardner
4.	Clark Gable	D.	Britt Ekland
5.	Michael Williams	E.	Carole Lombard
6.	Tony Curtis	F.	Carrie Fisher
7.	Frank Sinatra	G.	Catherine Zeta Jones
8.	Laurence Olivier	H.	Connie Booth
9.	Prince Rainier	I.	Elizabeth Taylor
10.	Paul Newman	J.	Grace Kelly
11.	Peter Sellars	K.	Janet Leigh
12.	John Thaw	L.	Joanne Woodward
13.	Robert Wagner	M.	Judi Dench
14.	Richard Burton	N.	Lauren Bacall
15.	Warren Beatty	O.	Lucille Ball
16.	Steve McQueen	P.	Marilyn Monroe
17.	Paul Simon	Q.	Mia Farrow
18.	Michael Douglas	R.	Natalie Wood
19.	Arthur Miller	S.	Pauline Collins
20.	Mickey Rooney	T.	Sheila Hancock
21.	John Cleese	U.	Vivien Leigh

Answers: 1S, 2O, 3N, 4E, 5M, 6K, 7Q, 8U, 9J, 10L, 11D, 12T, 13R, 14I, 15B, 16A, 17F, 18G, 19P, 20C, 21H

An autumn secret

BY: MARION FELLOWS

Rosie's husband is behaving strangely and her suspicions are aroused

Rosie shivered: there was a definite nip in the air and a solitary leaf fluttering down from the apple tree signified the onset of autumn, her favourite season.

'I wonder if they have autumn in Australia?' she speculated, her thoughts turning to her daughter Jenny who lived there with her young family.

In the photos she sent, life was all sunshine and barbecues. It looked lovely but in Rosie's view it would be hard to beat a crisp, frosty morning.

Back in her cosy kitchen, she looked again at her treasured photos, blinking back a few tears at the sight of her two grandchildren, Tommy and Laura, who she had yet to meet and hold close.

Busying herself with dusting and polishing, Rosie cast her mind back to the first time she and Jim had set eyes on the cottage. It had been in such a state of neglect that her parents tried to dissuade the eager couple from buying it. But Rosie and Jim had fallen totally in love with each other and the cottage and weren't to be put off.

Over the years Jim had worked tirelessly, exposing old beams and renovating the lovely old place to make Honeysuckle Cottage a home once again.

Jim put his head around the door: "Just off to the allotment, love, I'll take the car as my poor old legs aren't what they used to be."

Rosie watched his car turn into the lane feeling that there was something not quite right. She couldn't quite say how or why, but her Jim had changed.

For the last month he'd left the cottage every morning, always taking the car and not, as in the past, his trusty old bike. At first Rosie thought nothing of it but she noticed that when he came home, laden with home-grown vegetables, he just plonked himself down in the armchair and was not his usual chatty self.

He no longer made Rosie laugh at the antics of his fellow

She couldn't say how or why, but her Jim had changed

allotment holders, Fred and Joe, or argued with the TV when he disagreed with some viewpoint or other. Instead, he fell asleep, only to be roused by Rosie reminding him to drink up his cocoa.

If Jim was going to be out all day again, Rosie decided she would go out, too. She would use her recently acquired pensioner's pass to catch the bus into town for some retail therapy.

"Good morning, young lady,'" joked the bus driver, "off to spend the old man's money at the market, are we?"

But they had hardly gone a mile, when the bus was flagged down by a policeman who boarded the vehicle and spoke to the driver. He turned to his passengers and announced: "I'm sorry, folks, there is a burst water main further along this road so we'll have to make a detour round the Marylands estate. It'll give us chance to see how the other half live!"

Known locally as Millionaires' Row, the Marylands estate was very exclusive. Rosie settled back ready to enjoy her bird's eye view of gracious living.

There was no envy in her heart for no grand residence could compare with her little cottage. Then she sat forward suddenly – surely that was Jim's car parked in that gravelled driveway?

The bus slowed down and she caught sight of Jim himself, ringing the doorbell and being welcomed in by a smiling young woman.

A tidal wave of emotions swept over her. Rosie struggled to compose herself but the rest of the morning passed in a daze as she walked through the market, oblivious to the hustle and bustle.

Sitting in the bus on her way home, Rosie made up her mind to confront Jim that evening, however painful the outcome might be.

She reeled back in disbelief

ILLUSTRATION: KATE DAVIES

Walking up the front path, Rosie saw that Jim's car was already there. Before she could insert her key, the door flew open and Jim demanded: "Where have you been?"

Taking her by the arm, he almost dragged her inside. Before she could take her coat off, he thrust an envelope into her hand.

"This is for you," he said.

Nervously, Rosie opened it, her hands trembling. The contents spilled onto the hall table and she reeled back in disbelief. Two airline tickets to Australia!

"Look at the date," instructed Jim.

"The twenty-sixth of October," Rosie read out, falteringly.

"That's our ruby wedding anniversary, Rosie," Jim said softly.

"But how ever…"

"How did I manage to afford it? Well, these last few weeks I've been doing some renovation work on one of the houses on the Marylands estate. It belongs to Harry Baker who owns that chain of bookies. Old Fred was placing a bet when he heard he was looking for someone with the right skills."

He took Rosie's hand: "It's

been hard keeping it from you, love, but I desperately wanted it to be a surprise. A celebration of our life together."

Just then the phone rang and Rosie answered it. It was Jenny.

"Oh Mum, I'm so happy!" she exclaimed. "It's going to be the best Christmas ever. Tommy and Laura are so excited about seeing their grandparents. Isn't it wonderful?"

Tears filled Rosie's eyes: "It certainly is wonderful, darling," and looking over at Jim who was carefully pouring a celebratory glass of wine, she added: "and so is your father."

Thursday 1	Monday 12
Friday 2	Tuesday 13
Saturday 3	Wednesday 14
Sunday 4	Thursday 15
Monday 5	Friday 16
Tuesday 6	Saturday 17
Wednesday 7	Sunday 18
Thursday 8	Monday 19
Friday 9	Tuesday 20
Saturday 10	Wednesday 21
Sunday 11	Thursday 22

Friday **23**	Wednesday **28**
Saturday **24** <div align="right">United Nations' Day</div>	Thursday **29**
Sunday **25** <div align="right">British Summer Time (BST) ends</div>	Friday **30**
Monday **26**	Saturday **31** <div align="right">Hallowe'en</div>
Tuesday **27**	

PIC: REX FEATURES

Behind the Scenes

Every Which Way But Loose, 1978

Who's the star here, and who's the co-star? This cute photograph of Clint Eastwood and Clyde the orangutan was obviously taken during a script consultation between the two stars during the making of Every Which Way But Loose in 1978.

Clint plays trucker Philo Beddoe who, along with his friend Orville, and Clyde, take off to look for Philo's true love, Lynn, played by Sondra Locke – with whom Eastwood lived from 1976 to 1988.

Clint first made his name as Rowdy Yates in the long running TV series, Rawhide, then became an international star in Sergio Leone's trilogy of 'Spaghetti westerns' and as Inspector 'Dirty' Harry Callahan in the Dirty Harry movies. So this comedy film was quite a departure for the tough guy

and all-action hero – and a surprise to the film industry. But it became a success, along with its 1980 sequel Any Which Way You Can.

And Mr Eastwood went on to great things as a film director, including The Bridges of Madison County, Million Dollar Baby and The Outlaw Josey Wales.

Schooldays remembered

Top: Edna's first school photo
Above: Edna and Gordon,
aged 10 and 11

I was five when I started at the Methodist Junior School in Leyland in 1947, and I remember my first day well. Mum walked to the school gates with me and my brother, Gordon, who was 11 months older than I and had started school the year before, so he knew his way around.

When Mum had gone Gordon looked worried, saying he'd have to leave me here, as this was the girls' playground, and he walked away.

I didn't like this idea and felt very alone, so I ran after him. A little boy at the entrance to the boys' playground stopped me and said: "You can't come in." "I'll go where I want," I said, pushing him out of the way.

The teacher looking after the new starters asked me if I was all right, and I told her I thought it was a silly idea having separate playgrounds.

She smiled at my outburst, but this was only one of many.

I found playing with sand, shells and beanbags a bit boring after making pretend motor cars and jumping over the brook with Gordon.

I very often disrupted the other children and ended up standing in the corner with my hands on my head until lunchtime. But after a while I toed the line and began to enjoy learning and being friends with other children beside my brother.

I had school dinners and wasn't a fussy eater, and I was the only one in my class who would eat fish. I would eat anything except the raisins in the semolina pudding – they made me feel sick the way they slithered down my throat when I swallowed them.

**Edna Lydiate,
Leyland, Lancs**

My Grandparents

Nanny Turner

Mary Martha Morgan Bush, my most wonderful Grandmother, was born in 1888. She came from a poor family, but a Salvation Army friend of Mary's mother offered to 'foster' Mary, so she became used to good clothes and toys for a short while.

However, her kind, new 'mother' died not long after fostering, so Mary went back to her family again. When she was 18 she married Henry Turner and had nine children.

In 1919 Mary caught Spanish influenza and was never as strong afterwards, developing rheumatoid arthritis and becoming very deformed. She spent 38 years in a wheelchair and though in great pain, never once complained.

Even though she was ill so often, Nanny would often rally when told a piece of good news, such as a birth or wedding. The day I wrote to tell her she was to have a new great-grandchild, she sadly died, and never knew.

Joan Pape, Percy Main, North Shields

Cookery for you

PEA, BROCCOLI AND MINT SOUP

Serves 4

- ◆ 1 tablespoon olive oil
- ◆ 25 g (1 oz) butter
- ◆ 1 medium white onion, finely chopped
- ◆ 1 garlic clove, finely chopped
- ◆ 400 ml (14 fl oz) chicken stock
- ◆ 400 g (13 oz) shelled peas
- ◆ 110 g (4 oz) broccoli florets
- ◆ Juice of 1 lemon
- ◆ Salt and cracked black pepper
- ◆ Small bunch of mint, shredded
- ◆ Extra virgin olive oil, for drizzling

1 Melt the oil and the butter in a large saucepan, add the onion and garlic and cook over a gentle heat until soft, about 10 minutes.

2 Add the chicken stock and bring to the boil. Add the peas and broccoli and cook until soft, around 5 minutes.

3 Remove half the soup and blend in a food processor, then add back into the rest of the liquid.

4 Add the lemon juice, season and stir in the mint.

5 Serve in warmed bowls with a drizzle of extra virgin olive oil.

Recipe courtesy Tenderstem® broccoli, www.tenderstem.co.uk

Colourful climbers
Rose 'Kew Rambler'

Although this lovely rambling rose looks great when in full flower during the summer – it produces an abundance of single rose-pink blooms similar to those of wild roses with a musky scent – it's also wonderful during autumn when covered with masses of small red hips that last many weeks. Extremely reliable, it makes bushy growth and can be allowed to scramble through trees. Height 7m.

▎THAT'S INTERESTING...

The notes on the lines of a treble clef in music are: E, G, B, D, F. A good way to remember them if you're learning to read music is: 'Eat Good Bread Dear Father'

TOP TIP

Keep a lookout over the year for which company is offering the cheapest gas and electricity – and don't be afraid to switch!

Healthier for longer!

Have your chips – and eat them! Hurrah – chips just got healthier. Scientists have discovered that pre-soaking potatoes in water before frying them could reduce levels of acrylamide – a chemical which could cause cancer. Be super healthy by leaving the skins on, sprinkling with olive oil and baking them instead.

Cookery for you
CHOCOLATE STACK

Serves 8

For the stack
- 110 g (4 oz) self-raising flour
- 2 teaspoons baking powder
- 25 g (1 oz) cocoa
- 8 tablespoons granulated Splenda®
- 3 tablespoons dried skimmed milk powder
- 2 tablespoons ground rice
- 2 eggs, beaten
- 7 tablespoons vegetable oil
- 100 ml (4 fl oz) skimmed milk mixed with 4 tablespoons water
- 1 teaspoon vanilla essence

For the icing
- 110 g (4 oz) dark chocolate, melted
- 4 tablespoons granulated Splenda® dissolved in 2 teaspoons warm water
- 50 g (2 oz) spread
- Dusting of cocoa, to serve

1 Preheat oven to 180°C/350°F/Gas Mark 4. Line a 30.5cm x 23 cm swiss roll tin (12 in x 9 in) with baking paper.

2 Sift the flour, baking powder and cocoa into a bowl. Stir in the Splenda®, dried milk and ground rice.

3 Add the rest of ingredients and mix together. Spoon into the tin and level.

4 Bake for 10-15 minutes, or until a skewer comes out clean. Tip onto a wire rack and peel away the paper. Use a sharp knife to trim the edges, leave to cool.

5 For the icing, mix together all the ingredients and beat until smooth.

6 Divide the cake into three equal pieces. Spread a third of the icing over and repeat process twice again, forming a stack. Dust with cocoa.

Recipe courtesy Splenda®, www.splenda.co.uk

My Grandparents

My Grandpa served in the First World War and could neither read nor write, but he knew plenty about the land and the sea.

Grandma kept chickens, goats and pigs, and Grandpa grew most vegetables – and I loved to help them with the animals and crops – what a happy childhood.

The photo with my Grandpa was taken when I went up to one of his fields to show him my new Sunday School anniversary outfit – a blue skirt with matching waistcoat and white blouse, and a new pair of sandals. Having his photograph taken was rare for Grandpa and he loved it.

Eileen Le Lacheur, Forest, Guernsey

Eileen and her Granddad

Healthier for longer!

Drink fruit juice – or vegetable juice every morning – it could help to fight off Alzheimer's. It's the antioxidant vitamins packed into every glass of fresh juice that are thought to help keep your brain healthy.

THAT'S INTERESTING...

If you've had a hard day and are finding it hard to unwind, sit down and sigh deeply three times – and take your time over them. Sighing will help you relax.

Schooldays remembered

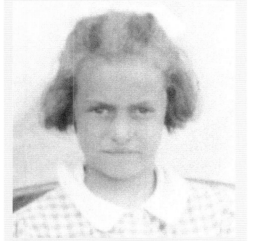

A rather pensive Pat at Bures School

I lived in the village of Bures in Suffolk, and I went to the village school at three-and-half years old, as my mother filled the milk bottles for the children to have at breaktime.

I had to sit at the end of the large classroom that had the sand table, the rocking horse and wooden bricks but I couldn't play, and had to be quiet as the teacher was very strict. I didn't fancy being five years old.

The only subjects I was interested in at school were art, needlework and country dancing. I also liked cookery, which was done in the headmaster's house – his wife taught us to clean and cook.

One day it was my turn to read out the ingredients for Maids of Honour and I forgot the flour. They looked a bit strange when they came out of the oven, but I didn't get into trouble!

Patricia Charman, Colchester, Essex

Meeting the stars

Joyce and Sir Jimmy

In July 1988 my husband and I were on holiday in Yorkshire with our two little dogs. We were visiting Bolton Abbey and stopped at the tea rooms for a cuppa. Sir Jimmy Savile was there and he spotted our dogs and made a fuss of them. We asked if we could take a photograph of him, and he said, 'We ought to find some better scenery'. And this photo is the result – Jim certainly fixed it for us that day!

Joyce Parrish, Burton-on-Trent, Staffs

Colourful climbers
Billardiera longiflora

A very desirable climber from Tasmania, Billardiera longiflora is hardy enough to be grown outside in the mildest parts of the country, producing greenish-yellow or cream, bell-shaped flowers that are indigo inside. These are a joy during the summer but are followed by attractive, almost metallic, purple berries during the autumn. Sow seed in March and plant out seedlings when all danger of frost has passed. Seeds available from Thompson and Morgan at www,thompson-morgan.com

TOP TIP

Don't be tempted to use washing up liquid to wash your car, as some may contain salts which harm metal.

Cookery for you

Colourful climbers

Abutilon megapotamicum

If you really want to bring your garden alive this summer, then the unusual climber Abutilon megapotamicum should be on your list. Reliably producing arching shoots of green leaves and amazing yellow and crimson flowers that resemble hot-air balloons, it makes an excellent container plant but requires winter protection in frost-prone areas if grown outside. Seeds are available from Thompson and Morgan at www,thompson-morgan.com

THAT'S INTERESTING...

Britain's most popular chocolate bar is Cadbury Dairy Milk.

Healthier for longer!

Prevent dementia – regular moderate exercise such as walking or cycling could reduce your risk of age-related memory decline by up to 27 per cent. Try to do 30 minutes three to five times a week.

WHOLEWHEAT PASTA WITH CHEESE SAUCE

Serves 4

◆ 300 g (11 oz) wholewheat fusilli or penne pasta
◆ 50 g (2 oz) butter
◆ 50 g (2 oz) wholemeal flour
◆ 570 ml (1 pint) semi–skimmed milk
◆ 110 g (4 oz) Cheddar cheese, grated
◆ 75 g (3 oz) wholemeal breadcrumbs

1 Cook pasta according to pack instructions, drain and return to the pan. Preheat the grill to medium.
2 Meanwhile, melt the butter in a small saucepan and stir in the flour, cook gently for 1 minute. Gradually stir in the milk. Bring to the boil, stirring until thickened, then stir in the cheese until melted, season to taste. Stir into the pasta and transfer to an ovenproof dish.
3 Sprinkle with breadcrumbs and place under the grill until golden.
4 Serve with a fresh crispy green salad.

Tip: For a boost of vitamin C, roast 250 g (9 oz) cherry tomatoes drizzled with a little olive oil for 15 minutes and stir into the pasta with the cheese sauce.

Recipe courtesy www.wholegraingoodness.com

My Grandparents

U ntil I was seven, my parents and I lived with Mum's parents, Arthur and Elizabeth Billington, in Oldham. When my brother was born and we moved, I still spent lots of time at Grandma and Granddad's.

They were both characters, Grandma tiny and feisty, Granddad, a born story teller, who had a lifelong passion for two things; radical politics and toffees.

I was about 12, and Grandma sent me upstairs to fetch something down for her. I hadn't been in the back bedroom for a long time and I noticed a white carrier bag on top of the wardrobe.

Intrigued, I climbed on the chair to have a look and got quite a shock to find what must have been six pounds of sweets. I'd found Granddad's secret stash of goodies. No wonder he always had a pocketful of sweets which made him very popular with the local kids.

Arthur and Elizabeth with granddaughter, Shirley

I hurried back down to tell Grandma of my find. She laughed and said we'd play a trick on Granddad, and she hid half the sweets in her drawer and warned me not to say a word.

Poor Granddad went round the house for some time with a puzzled look on his face until Grandma finally came clean and put him out of his misery. Always a good sport, he laughed and said he'd get even with her one day!

Shirley Hall, Oldham, Lancs

Schooldays remembered

B e green and recycle, we're told – in 1947, it wasn't a lifestyle choice but a necessity. Precious clothing coupons were used for new liberty bodices, stout school knickers and scratchy wool socks. And like every other mum, mine had to fall back on her needlework skills for the rest.

School itself was improvised, the Baptist Chapel we went to on Sunday was our school on Monday, trestle tables and benches replacing the chapel chairs.

Paper was in short supply, so some old slates and pencils were dug up from somewhere, and only when we were able to form small, tidy letters were we promoted to working on paper – and we had to use every inch of it.

Only two sheets of toilet paper could be taken for each visit to the outdoor

A school photo of Francis, in 1948

toilet; the toilet roll hung from a string in the lobby. One day I was feeling defiant and helped myself to three sheets but unfortunately I was spotted by the school bully, a big boy of six.

He told me the police would be calling at my house that night. After school, I crept home, unable to eat my tea or explain what a dreadful thing I'd done. It took my mum several hours to wrench the terrible truth from me. I couldn't understand why she laughed, before reassuring me that I wouldn't be going to prison.

I remember my early schooldays with pleasure and realise how very resourceful our teachers were and what a wonderful education we received despite the shortage of materials.

Frances Williams,
Basingstoke, Hants

Cookery for you

STRAWBERRY MASCARPONE CHEESECAKE

Serves 8-10

- ◆ 200 g (7 oz) shortbread biscuits, crushed
- ◆ 25 g (1 oz) butter, melted
- ◆ 405 g can Carnation Condensed Milk Light
- ◆ 2 x 250 g (9 oz) tubs mascarpone cheese
- ◆ Juice of 2 large lemons
- ◆ 450 g (1 lb) strawberries
- ◆ 2 tablespoons strawberry jam

1 Mix the crushed biscuits with the melted butter, then lightly press the mixture into a 20 cm (8 inch) lined and greased spring form tin in an even layer. Chill for 20 minutes.

2 Beat the condensed milk with the mascarpone cheese until mixture is smooth. Add the lemon juice and combine thoroughly.

3 In a blender or food processor, pulse half the strawberries with the jam until lightly crushed, leaving small pieces.

4 Spread half the cream mixture onto the biscuit base. Spoon over the crushed strawberries, and top with the remaining cream mixture. Chill for 4 hours.

5 Halve the remaining strawberries and arrange on top of the cheesecake.

Recipe courtesy Nestlé Carnation, www.carnation.co.uk

My Grandparents

When I was a child, my Grandmother and I would take large ivy leaves from the wall, soak them in vinegar, then place them on her legs and feet to relieve her rheumatism, and it seemed to work.

Grandma would also collect me from school at lunchtimes and prepare a Cremola pudding for my 'afters', then wash my hands and powder them with face powder to make sure they were dry. We'd walk back to school via the mews so that I could watch the horses being shod by the blacksmiths. This was in Paddington during the war.

My Grandma was such a sweet, gentle lady, who loved all her grandchildren equally.

Jo Masters, Tenterden, Kent

Jane Esther Jenkins, Jo's Grandma

Healthier for longer!

Forgive and forget – people who are able to let go of a grudge are much less likely to experience pain, anxiety, anger and depression than people who keep hanging on to their resentment say scientists.

TOP TIP

Try and avoid telephone numbers beginning with 0870 – they're very expensive.

THAT'S INTERESTING...

During the year to June 2007, American thriller writer James Patterson, became the most borrowed author from UK libraries.

Schooldays remembered

Anne in 1939

My schooldays were not particularly happy ones. I was a sickly child and was often kept home from school because of some childhood illness or other. My particular dread was waiting in line to be given cod liver oil and malt from a spoon. We were forced to take it and I can recall struggling valiantly to keep it down.

On Friday afternoon we were allowed to bring one of our own books to read. While the teacher went to the staff room to mark our books, one of the senior girls would look after us as we read. But the books were soon thrust aside in favour of well thumbed copies of the Beano and Dandy. We also loved Film Fun, Radio Fun and Enid Blyton's Sunny Stories, while the boys squabbled over copies of Hotspur and The Wizard.

My best friend at infant school was Cathy, none of the other children would play with her, or sit beside her as we all knew she had nits. Cathy was always hungry. Sometimes the teacher would give her an extra bottle of milk, and I would watch her push her grubby thumb through the hole in the cardboard lid to lift it off, licking with relish the underside that was thick with cream.

Cathy was a great friend to have in the schoolyard if there was a fight; she could pack a punch that would outdo any of the boys.

**Anne Menenez,
Stockton on Tees, Cleveland**

Colourful climbers
Dolichos

Astrange sounding climber it may be but Dolichos 'Ruby Moon' will get you talking, producing delicate purple flowers from July until October followed by dark maroon beans. It thrives in full sun and will cope in really hot positions where other climbers may struggle. A half-hardy annual, it's available as seed and can be sown during March and planted outside once all the frosts have passed. Height 3m. Available as seeds from Thompson and Morgan at www.thompson-morgan.com

Meeting the stars

In 1974 Frankie Laine, the singer famous for such songs as Answer Me and Jezebel, came over to England at the request of his appreciation society. The fan who organised it asked my husband, Glyn, and I if we would sit with Frankie after his shows, to help him with selling his albums. We met him on the first night, before the show, and couldn't believe we were actually in the presence of our hero!

We got to know him very well and had some fabulous times over the years but we'll always treasure that week in 1974 when we were part of his life.

Annette Walker, Henley-on-Arden, Warks

Glyn and Annette with Frankie

Schooldays remembered

Kay, aged seven

Contrary to popular myth, I actually enjoyed school meals. In the mid 1950s when I went to Eccleshill North Junior School from age 7-11, I remember vegetables served in white tureens with lids and we helped ourselves, and the mashed potato was fluffy and delicious!

At Eccleshill North Secondary School (late 1950s early 1960s) the food was also good – beef stew, cheese and onion pie, and a dessert which had a pastry base covered with jam, then firm cold custard topped with dessicated coconut, and hot custard poured over the top.

We had games twice a week, when we girls played netball and hockey in winter and tennis in summer. After games, we had the compulsory shower, when we had to follow each other through the shower, hair usually covered with a rain hat, then get dried and dressed, all in the space of about ten minutes.

It all seemed very hectic at the time, and woe betide us if we arrived at the next lesson with our blouse not tucked in properly or our tied not tied correctly.

Kay Spurr,
Kirkby Stephen, Cumbria

My Grandparents

Margaret and Henry, Margaret's Grandparents

Henry Shallcross was 20 years old, tall, dark, handsome and engaged to be married. He had everything he wanted, until one bright sunny morning while working at his older brother William's grocery shop in Everton, Liverpool, a heavy meat hook fell on his head and as a result, blinded him.

After the accident he went home to Little Barrow in Cheshire. His fiancée ended their engagement, and for many years he led a solitary life; his father and family encouraged him to become a master grocer and he ran the village shop.

The customers were amazed at how he could tell whoever came into the shop by their footsteps on the stone floor.

He first met his wife, my grandmother, Martha Jones, at the village pump. She was very shy of him at first, but they talked for a while, then she went home to her village, not telling him her name, or where she lived. Nobody knew who she was or where

she came from – Henry felt he must resign himself to bachelorhood for ever.

Then a few weeks later my Grandmother found herself in the grocer's shop doing errands for her father. Martha stood by the counter and couldn't believe who was standing right in front of her. He was thrilled even before she spoke because he knew it was Martha by the sound of her footsteps.

They immediately fell in love and married very soon after that meeting, and had five children.

Margaret A Turner, Frodsham, Cheshire

Cookery for you

PORK RAGU

Serves 4

- ◆ 1 teaspoon olive oil
- ◆ 1 onion, finely chopped
- ◆ 2 cloves garlic, crushed
- ◆ 450 g (1 lb) lean minced pork
- ◆ 3 rashers lean dry cured bacon
- ◆ 1 medium carrot, finely chopped
- ◆ 1 courgette, sliced
- ◆ 400 g can chopped tomatoes
- ◆ 2 teaspoons tomato purée

To serve
- ◆ 350g (12 oz) spaghetti
- ◆ 25g (1 oz) Parmesan cheese, to serve
- ◆ Fresh basil, for garnish

1 Fry the onions and garlic in the oil in a medium saucepan until soft. Add the mince and bacon and cook over a low heat until browned, about 4-6 minutes.

2 Increase the heat and cook the meat for 4-6 minutes or until browned.

3 Add the carrot, courgette, chopped tomatoes and tomato purée. Bring to the boil, cover and simmer for 25 minutes.

4 Serve with the cooked spaghetti, Parmesan shavings and roughly torn fresh basil.

Recipe courtesy LovePork, www.lovepork.co.uk

Colourful climbers
Pyracantha

A reliable plant that tolerates neglect, pyracantha produces clusters of small white flowers in spring, followed by bunches of orange, red or yellow berries in autumn. It thrives in sun or partial shade and copes with different soils. Although it berries best in sunshine, it will grow happily up walls of any aspect. It requires training – a rigid piece of trellis is essential – and looks better when pruned to shape. Plants widely available.

THAT'S INTERESTING...

The largest flower in the world, the rafflesia arnoldi, can weigh up to 7 kg (15 pounds) and grows only in Indonesia. When in bloom, it gives off a terrible smell.

TOP TIP

To avoid eye strain when knitting with dark coloured wool, cover your lap with a white piece of cloth. **Annette Chambers, London W6**

Healthier for longer!

Head for the hills – if you're thinking of taking a short holiday go somewhere hilly. Researchers in Greece found that people who live in hilly areas live longer than folk in the lowlands. This could be because the extra physical demands of walking over hilly terrain with less oxygen keeps them fitter.

Nottingham:
D H Lawrence Country

Mining history

DH Lawrence was brought up in the small mining community of Eastwood where his father was a miner. The terrace house where he was born in 1885, 8A Victoria Street, is now a museum that recreates the working-class life so vividly depicted in his first novel Sons and Lovers.

Nearby is the Durban House Heritage Centre which used to be the offices of the Barber Walker Mining Company where Lawrence went as a boy to collect his father's wages. After his death in France in 1930 his headstone was brought back to his birthplace and is on display in Eastwood library.

The more rural neighbouring parish of Greasley was well known to Lawrence and many of the locations he used in his books can still be seen. He was a regular visitor to Haggs Farm where his friend

Jessie Chambers lived. She became Miriam in Sons and Lovers and the farm's name was changed to Willey Farm. Moorgreen Reservoir became the scene of a drowning in Women in Love. Greasley church, St Mary's, is mentioned in his fiction but today is more famous for Mintons Tea Rooms in the church hall.

Lawrence is also commemorated in the city of Nottingham where he attended the High School and later studied to be a teacher at Nottingham University. A life-size bronze statue of the writer stands in the university's grounds.

One of the oldest fairs in Britain, the Nottingham Goose Fair, is held for three days annually in October.

Letters led to love

A fine romance

An army corporal played Cupid for
Mr Ernest Hughes of Cheadle

My twenty-first birthday in 1942 was spent in a lean-to in a field near the town of Bougie in North Africa where I was camped with my mobile engineer unit.

When the mail finally reached us, among my birthday cards was a 'Dear John' letter from my fiancée.

I confided in a corporal who told me to 'get on with life'. He said that his sister was in the ATS and she was sending some names and addresses of women who would like to have pen friends.

All the names went into a hat and I picked

out Private G M Roberts whose address was in Caernarfon, North Wales. I couldn't write much as our letters were censored but I did say both my parents were of Welsh descent.

The letter was pushed to the back of my mind as we landed on the beach at Salerno in Italy in September 1943. When we arrived in Naples, the mail caught up with us and there was a letter from Miss Gwen Mary Roberts who explained she had been discharged from the army to nurse her mother.

I wrote to her weekly and in 1954 I was posted to Palestine and in November granted one month's leave in the UK. I spent a week with my parents but couldn't wait to keep my promise to go and see Gwen. We met for the first time on a very cold morning on the platform of Caernarfon station.

We had kept no secrets from each other in our letters and after an hour in each other's company we both knew we had made the right choice. We were married by special licence on December 23 1945.

The next step

Barbara Bignall had always loved the countryside but thought that 'real walking' was for hardy types. But then came a two-mile nature ramble...

I'd read that walking kept the weight down, improves our sleep and is good for our health, but my response was always, 'Where do I start?' or '10,000 steps a day? They must be joking'.

But it is possible, and if I started walking in my mid-50s after my daughters – and husband – had flown the nest – just about anyone can. (As long as your doctor gives you the okay.)

As caravanners, our family had been on short walks from campsites but I longed to put on a rucksack and join the groups zig-zagging their way through the Derbyshire hills and the Lake District. Perhaps, one day I could walk in the Swiss mountains…

On my own, older and heavier, I saw an advert in the library for a two-mile ramble. Now, two miles in a car passes before you can glance at the speedometer – how would I cope on two feet? No problem, though, with stops while the ranger explained about plants and berries. I was hooked.

The next step was to join a rambling club. My rambling holidays abroad started when I felt confident enough to walk most days of the week.

And it soon became clear that my new hobby was not all about exercise and pretty views – there's the social side. You can chat away

to many different people and it was especially good to hear how other people coped with divorce – I wasn't the only 'single'.

Rambling certainly doesn't have to be costly, although you need stout footwear and a rain jacket. Neither does it have to be the equivalent of a commando course – the local weekend papers give details of walks run by various organisations.

I meet up most weeks for short walks with two ramblers who live in my adopted county of Northamptonshire, which brings me to my other hobby – writing – which came about through walking.

Having left school at 14 without any qualifications, being a writer seemed unachievable, but I started writing letters to magazine editors, followed by camp site reports.

I was well into bus pass years when Family Camping was published. I still get a thrill thinking about my book in major bookshops, as well as in the library.

In my seventies and thinking of retiring, I was asked by Countryside Books to write, Drive and Stroll in Northamptonshire

Above: Barbara in San Jacinto Wilderness Park, California
Middle: Walking in the grounds of Kirby Hall, Northants. Top: Evia, Greece

– each walk between three and five miles. Addicted to writing and walking, I couldn't refuse!

So I'd achieved two dreams in one. Walking the hills and dales of our own beautiful countryside, and in countries I'd only seen on television and having books published.

Season's greetings

BY: LINDA POVEY

How can single mum Karen afford a truly happy Christmas?

Karen zipped up Amy's anorak. "Now put your hood up," she told her. "It's really cold out today."

"Do I have to?" Amy's big sigh made Karen smile. "Yes, you do."

She took Amy's gloved hand as they set off down the street. She wished she could buy herself a new winter coat but right now her main worry was how to afford at least some of the presents Amy had on her Christmas wish list.

How could anyone explain to a six-year-old who believed in Father Christmas that it was really Mummy who had to fork out?

Deep in thought, she failed to see old Mr. Cook coming through his front gate.

She wished she could buy herself a new coat

"Watch where you're going!" he yelled as they collided.

"My fault, Mr Cook," Karen said, "I wasn't looking where I was going."

"That's obvious," he grumbled.

"Freezing, isn't it?" Karen said.

But the old man wasn't in any mood for polite conversation. "Huh," he grunted.

"Well, must be getting on," Karen said brightly, adding, "Bah, humbug," when they were out of earshot.

"What do you mean, Mummy?"

"That's what Scrooge used to say. He meant he didn't like Christmas."

"I love Christmas," Amy said. "Don't you?"

"Oh yes," Karen told her. And she did. Though it wasn't the easiest of time of the year for a single parent.

In Hadley's department store, Amy piped up: "Mummy, can I see Father Christmas? Please! Please!"

They joined the queue for Santa's grotto.

"What's that?" Karen asked.

"It's my list for Santa," Amy said, opening it up.

Karen groaned inwardly as she read over Amy's shoulder. The spelling was wonky, but the words were clear. So far, she had bought just one present on the list, a stroller for Amy's doll. And she'd had to save hard for that.

Karen and Amy were ushered through the curtains by a middle-aged fairy.

"Hello there, little girl. And what's your name?"

Karen stopped in her tracks. She knew that voice. It was Mr Cook. An unlikelier Father Christmas she couldn't imagine.

Mercifully, Amy didn't recognise him. She was lost in the magic of Santa.

"Amy," she told him, with a shy smile.

"That's a nice name. And what would you like for Christmas?"

"I've written a list so you can remember." Amy gave him the piece of paper.

"Well, that makes things a whole lot easier – I'm sure we can manage to find most of these," Mr Cook said.

Karen was incensed at his thoughtlessness. The next day, when Amy was having tea at a friend's house, she marched round to confront the old man. Plucking up her courage, she rang the bell.

The door was opened slowly. "Hello," said Mr Cook, frowning, "what do you want?"

Full of charm as ever, Karen thought. "I won't come in," she told him. "I just wanted to say I think it's most irresponsible of you, in your guise as Santa Claus, to promise children Christmas presents their parents can't necessarily afford."

He looked uncomfortable. "I always tell them I might not be able to get hold of all they ask for," he defended himself.

"Well, in my daughter's case, she's only going to get one thing on her list," Karen said angrily. "Do you

ILLUSTRATION: KATE DAVIES

have any idea how difficult it is for a single mother to make ends meet?"

"It's not easy for a pensioner, either," Mr Cross replied huffily. "That's why I took the Santa job."

"Then you ought to understand," Karen snapped, as she walked away feeling little satisfaction.

On Christmas Eve, Karen wrapped up the last of the stocking fillers and placed them in a pillow-case. She was about to take them upstairs when she heard a knock at the back door.

'Strange', she thought. Tentatively, she opened the door, leaving the chain on. There was no one there.

She was about to close the door again when she spotted a large cardboard box on the step.

Taking off the chain she went outside and lifted the lid. Inside were various wrapped parcels with labels which read: 'To Amy, from Father Christmas'.

Blinking back tears, Karen carried the box indoors.

On Christmas morning, Karen rang Mr Cook's doorbell once again.

"Merry Christmas!" she said, when he appeared.

"Merry Christmas to you," he replied.

"We just wondered what you were doing for Christmas lunch," she said.

"I've got a bit of chicken," he told her.

"You're going to be alone?"

"I usually am – no family, you know – but I'll be all right."

"We've got a small turkey; there will be plenty for three. Would you like to join us?"

Mr Cook's habitual frown relaxed into a smile: "That's very kind, I'd love to."

After lunch, he stayed on, chatting to Karen and helping Amy play with her new toys.

Karen guessed he had spent all the money he'd earned as Santa on those presents. How could she ever repay him? But she knew the answer to that. She and Amy could become the family he didn't have.

After he'd left, Karen got a sleepy Amy ready for bed. She said: "Mr Cook isn't like Scrooge any more, is he, Mummy?"

Karen stroked her daughter's hair. "No, love. More like Father Christmas." She laughed at Amy's puzzled look. "I'll explain when you're older," she promised.

Sunday

1

All Saints' Day

Monday

2

Tuesday

3

Wednesday

4

Thursday

5

Guy Fawkes' Night

Friday

6

Saturday

7

Sunday

8

Remembrance Sunday

Monday

9

Tuesday

10

Wednesday

11

Armistice Day

Thursday

12

Friday

13

Saturday

14

Lord Mayor's Show, London

Sunday

15

Monday

16

Tuesday

17

Wednesday

18

Thursday

19

Friday

20

Saturday

21

Sunday

22

Monday **23**	Friday **27**
Tuesday **24**	Saturday **28**
Wednesday **25**	Sunday **29** Advent Sunday
Thursday **26**	Monday **30** St Andrew's Day

PIC: REX FEATURES

Behind the Scenes

The Madwoman of Chaillot, 1968

Now there's a sight you wouldn't have seen very often – no, not the athletic Katharine Hepburn on a bike, but Director Bryan Forbes giving her a push start... a great light moment in the making of The Madwoman of Chaillot in 1968.

The film was adapted from a satire by the French dramatist, Jean Giraudoux, and it follows the story of Countess Aurelia, who puts up a fight against four corrupt authoritarian figures who find oil in the centre of Paris. Always plain speaking in real life, it seemed that Katharine Hepburn was perfect casting...

Director Bryan Forbes started his career as an actor, then began writing for the screen, notably the screenplay for The League of Gentlemen, with Jack Hawkins and Richard Attenborough. He made his directorial debut in 1961 with Whistle Down The Wind, starring Hayley Mills.

Cookery for you

MACADAMIA ROCKY ROAD

Makes 12

- ◆ 90 g (3½ oz) raw macadamia halves
- ◆ 200 g (7 oz) mini marshmallows
- ◆ 75 g (3 oz) glacé cherries, chopped
- ◆ 30 g (1 oz) desiccated coconut (optional)
- ◆ 500g (18 oz) milk chocolate

1 Mix together the macadamias, marshmallows, cherries and coconut and scatter over the base of a lined lamington tin.
2 Melt the chocolate and pour evenly over the top, smoothing the top.
3 Refrigerate until set, then cut into pieces with a hot sharp knife.
4 These can be stored in a sealed container in a cool place, or the refrigerator for up to 2 weeks.

Recipe courtesy Macadamia Advice Centre, www.Macadamia.org.uk

My Grandparents

My Grandmother's father was the inn keeper at the Dusty Miller pub in Wakefield, and my Grandma Pearson may have been born there.

When I was a schoolgirl, it was a weekend treat to go and stay with Gran. My brother and I slept in an large old brass bedstead, and I can recall a picture and a Bible passage which hung on the wall over the bed head. There was a white chamber pot underneath, in case we were caught short in the night!

Gran used to get up early, before anyone stirred, so that she could clear the old ashes and light the fire in the old black range. Gran also had an early electric cooker, and the delicious smell of frying eggs and bacon wafted through to the living room as we came down for breakfast.

On Sunday, the family would sit round the table for a big roast beef dinner

Grandma Pearson outside her back door

with Yorkshire puddings, and tinned fruit salad and bread and butter for dessert. Her sheepdog, Lassie, slept outside in a heavy wooden kennel which had lino nailed to the roof to keep it rainproof.

Margaret Humphries, Pudsey, Leeds

Healthier for longer!

Wash your hands – and disinfect your surfaces regularly if you want to protect yourself from harmful winter bugs. Spend at least 20 seconds washing your hands, with liquid soap and dry them thoroughly – bugs love warm, damp hands.

THAT'S INTERESTING...

In England the first recorded display of fireworks took place in 1486 during the wedding of King Henry VII.

Colourful climbers
Vitis coignetiae

Commonly called the Crimson glory vine, this ornamental plant makes a magnificent climber where it has plenty of room to spread. The large rounded leaves may reach 30cm in diameter and are dimpled, making them attractive throughout the summer. In autumn they turn fiery shades of red, gold and orange – a great sight as bonfire night approaches. It enjoys fertile, well-drained, chalky soils in sunny or partial shade, and may reach 15m in height. Plants widely available.

TOP TIP

Adding vinegar to the water when you poach an egg helps the egg white to seal quickly.

Meeting the stars

When my brother Vic was little he loved the song The Tennessee Waltz, so when Pearl Carr and Teddy Johnson came to the Cardiff New Theatre I took him to see them.

As I collected autographs, we went to the stage door after the show. When Teddy asked Vic if he enjoyed the show, he said: "Yes, but you didn't sing The Tennessee Waltz."

At that, they both sang it there and then for him, and made his day. Pearl and Teddy had just become engaged, so Vic and I were among the first to congratulate them.

June Mead, Wickford, Essex

Teddy Johnson and Pearl Carr

PIC: REX FEATURES

Schooldays remembered

'Big' school was a male-free zone, apart from the gardener and the caretaker, neither of whom were the stuff of young girls' dreams.

The school grounds were enormous and backed up on to a park with a deep ditch inside the fence. The ditch was used by groups of us bagging a spot for our den. First, we placed large branches across the gap, then smaller ones, and twigs, then leaves and finally, earth. This was beaten down, making the roof of our den tough enough to stand on, and peer over into the park.

The swings were the top favourite at break. The bliss in summer when you swung back and forth with your eyes closed, and rainbow colours flickering across your eyelids.

On rainy days, we played jacks in the assembly hall, collecting splinters from the parquet floor along our little fingers. We danced, too, to the gramophone; the waltz and the quickstep, taking turns at being the boy.

My favourite school pastime was 'swappies' – we exchanged greetings cards. A fancy one with gold and silver, or one with sparkle on merited two cards in exchange. I wish I'd kept them – they would be a collector's delight now.

Valerie Loudon, Bridport, Dorset

Schooldays remembered

Off to school for Murie

One of the happiest days of my life was when I heard that I'd won a Scholarship to go to Slough High School for Girls, to follow in my big sister's footsteps.

The school I'd attended from five years old was right opposite our house, but now all that was going to change. The High School was three miles away, and I was to go on my bicycle. Eventually the first day dawned, and I set off with a friend, Joy, our bikes clean and shining, and us resplendent in our new uniforms.

And full uniform had to be worn at all times, including hats when outside school. No jewellery of any description, and no make up. Hair had to be off your face, no long fringes, and hair longer than just below the ears had to be tied back.

They were very happy days; we were given lots of encouragement to follow the subjects in which we were interested and did well. I was very lucky to have the guidance of a visiting doctor who came to teach the pre-nursing pupils. I wanted to do something medical, and she guided me into physiotherapy, for which I've always been grateful.

The photograph was taken by my father, as we set off for our first day at school.

**Muriel Aird,
Weymouth, Dorset**

My Grandparents

Mary and William, with Carole

My grandparents, Mary and William Wright met after the First World War. My Grandfather fought in the trenches and had a friend called Henry Bamford. They made a pact that if one of them was killed, the other would go to their family and tell them what happened.

My Grandmother was married to Henry and, when he was killed, my Grandfather was injured and spent 12 months in hospital.

When he recovered, he went to see my Grandma, as he'd promised Henry, and told her about how he knew him, and what had happened.

My Grandfather lived in Carlisle, my Grandmother in Preston – he worked on the railway and had a pass to go anywhere, so this is how they met, eventually fell in love, and were married in 1921.

**Carole Neville,
Axminster, Devon**

Cookery for you

WHOLEMEAL CHICKEN PASTIES

Serves 4

- ◆ 150 g (5 oz) wholemeal flour
- ◆ 150 g (5 oz) plain flour
- ◆ 150 g (5 oz) butter, diced
- ◆ 225 g (8 oz) roasted chicken breasts, diced
- ◆ 4 spring onions, chopped
- ◆ 50 g (2 oz) baby corn, cut into 1 cm (¹/₂ inch) slices
- ◆ 5 cherry tomatoes, chopped
- ◆ 4 tablespoons tomato pesto
- ◆ 150 ml (¹/₄ pint) milk, for brushing

1 Preheat the oven to 200°C/400°F/Gas Mark 6.
2 Place the flour and butter in a food processor and mix until fine breadcrumbs. Add 4 tablespoons of water and process until a soft dough forms. Knead gently, then cover the pastry with clingfilm and chill for 15 minutes.
3 Mix together the chicken, vegetables and pesto.
4 Roll out the pastry and cut 17cm (6½ in) circles and divide the chicken filling between them. Wet the pastry edges with water and fold over the pastry to seal in the filling, to make a pasty shape.
5 Place on a baking tray and brush with a little milk. Bake for 25-30 minutes.
6 Served immediately with boiled new potatoes and green beans.

Recipe courtesy www.wholegraingoodness.com

Colourful climbers
Clematis 'Radar Love'

Although this variety looks similar to the species C tangutica and C orientalis, the reflexed petals on its flowers are a marked improvement, opening them up to the casual observer. However, like its relatives, these are followed by wispy seed heads that look magical when covered in frost. It thrives in sun or partial shade and enjoys well-drained soil. It grows quickly but should be pruned back hard every March. Plants widely available.

TOP TIP
To remove a beetroot stain, soak a piece of bread in water and dab it on both sides of the cloth. The bread will quickly absorb the colour.
Kathryn Croft, Hayling Island, Hants

Healthier for longer!

Have a cuppa – it could help to combat type 2 diabetes. Scottish scientists have discovered compounds in black tea that behave in a similar way to insulin in the body. Go easy on the sugar though, or it could cancel out the benefits.

THAT'S INTERESTING...
The trumpet dates back to 2000 BC (when it was first used for signalling in Ancient China). It was made of everyday items such as a hollow piece of wood, a seashell, or an animal horn. The Egyptians followed by the Romans constructed the first trumpets using long brass tubes.

Cookery for you

CHRISTMAS CAKE AND BRANDY PARFAIT
Serves 6-8

- ◆ 397 g can Carnation condensed milk
- ◆ 450 ml (³/₄ pint) single cream
- ◆ 200 ml (8 fl oz) carton crème fraîche
- ◆ 1 tablespoon vanilla extract
- ◆ 3 tablespoons brandy
- ◆ 450 g (1 lb) Christmas cake, crumbled
- ◆ Cranberry compote, to serve (optional)

1 Line a 900 g (2 lb) pudding basin with a double layer of clingfilm.
2 In a large bowl, whisk together the condensed milk, crème fraîche, vanilla extract and brandy until smooth and creamy.
3 Pour the mixture into a shallow plastic box and freeze until slushy (2-3 hours). Beat with a fork, and then gently stir in the crumbled Christmas cake.
4 Pour mixture into the pudding basin, cover and freeze overnight.
5 When serving, turn out the parfait onto a serving plate and remove the clingfilm.
6 Accompany with a spoonful of cranberry compote: Fresh cranberries simmered until sticky in a syrup of sugar and water.

Recipe courtesy Nestlé Carnation www.carnation.co.uk

My Grandparents

My paternal grandparents, Dot and Bert, rented a huge Georgian farmhouse in Gran's home of Pill, near Bristol and I stayed there often, and it was much more exciting when it was without my parents.

Although no longer a working farm, the farmyard was still home to chickens and ducks. Granddad loved his ducks and they often waddled in until Gran shooed them out again.

There were always cats and dogs, too, and in the winter the cats would gather round the black-leaded fireplace in front of the roaring fire, until Granddad scattered them with a couple of blasts of the fire bellows.

For breakfast in winter Gran would make creamy smooth porridge on a paraffin-fuelled primus stove. And it was she who taught me to crochet.

Granddad had the most fantastic sense of humour. Always an early riser, he would bring cups of tea, but you never knew

Top: Dot and Bert in 1950
Above: Lesley's dolls house

whether you would get a proper teacup, a basin or an eggcup-full of tea, and it could be stirred with a tiny salt spoon or a tablespoon – or occasionally a teaspoon, if you were lucky!

Lesley Bennion, Stafford

▮ THAT'S INTERESTING...

R2, D2, the robot hero of the film Star Wars, was named after a piece of film editors' jargon – it means 'Reel 2, Dialogue 2'.

Healthier for longer!
Spend time with children – looking after grandchildren could give you a real youth boost. They'll keep your brain engaged and help you burn off a whole lot of calories.

Colourful climbers

Parthenocissus tricuspidata

If you want great autumn colour, then Parthenocissus tricuspidata is impossible to beat. Self-clinging – so no trellis is required – its lobed green leaves turn fiery shades of red, yellow, orange, scarlet and bronze as the nights draw in. Use it as a screen, as a climber or let it scramble among other shrubs. It enjoys full sun or partial shade and well-drained soils. Height 18m. Plants widely available.

TOP TIP
If you're not yet on a water meter, think about having one installed – you could make big savings on your water bill.

Meeting the stars

I was 14 in 1955 and living with my aunt and uncle in Whyteleafe when filming started on the film classic Reach For The Sky at nearby Kenley Aerodrome, and which starred Kenneth More as Douglas Bader.

Through a friend, we were able to go and watch the scramble scene from the hangars. We'd been watching flight formations of Spitfires and Hurricanes for days, so we were very excited about going close to the filming.

When the film crew were taking a break, we asked Kenneth More for his autograph, and he was so obliging and charming. He told us all to turn round and signed our books leaning on our backs. And I still have his autograph.

Lillian Dean, Kenley, Surrey

PIC: ITV/REX FEATURES

Schooldays remembered

Tap dancing Joyce

My London childhood is full of nostalgic, happy memories. Surprising, as my schoolfriends and I, from Chapel End Infants School, were wartime children, familiar with the frequent sound of air-raid sirens calling us to take shelter.

Among my treasured memories are my tap dancing days at the Lynn Academy School of Dance, St James Street – I just loved it! Each year we took part in a big concert at The Pavilion in Lloyds Park, Walthamstow. I remember doing one routine as a solo. Having curly hair just like Shirley Temple – who was all the rage at that time – I tap danced and sang one of her songs. Luckily our Mums were clever at sewing and made us our pretty dresses, in spite of the clothes rationing.

The audience was packed with mums, dads, grandparents, aunts and uncles, it was such a big occasion for all the family. Those happy times have never been forgotten, so that even today I'm still tap dancing!

Joyce Dowds, Bridgwater, Somerset

Schooldays remembered

Above: Three-year-old Wyn
Left: Wyn in 1950

I was born in 1930. We lived in Hoghton, a scattered village comprising several small communities between Blackburn and Preston.

The village school was opposite the church with the Travellers' Rest at the gate. This stone shelter was where people would rest, having reached the top of a long haul from Preston before carrying on to Blackburn or Bolton.

I lived a mile from school and church but we were only allowed to use it if it was raining or snowing. What did God give you legs for?

There were three teachers, the headmaster Mr Burns, Miss Illsley and Mrs Bible for the middle group. What a most inappropriate name for that woman, my knees still knock after all these years. She always had her ruler in her hand with which she would rap our knuckles; she brought blood when used end on.

The school building was very high and stone cold. We took our dinner which we then gave to the older girls to warm up in the huge black oven in Mr Burns' room. Trust a man to have the only warm place in the school!

Wyn Crook, Orpington, Kent

My Grandparents

When we were children, mother always took us to see our Grandmother, Alice, who lived in Penge, south east London, on Sunday afternoons. Years later, one of our errands was to take a jug and buy her some stout, being very careful not to spill any on the way back. We were always rewarded with cakes and drinks.

When war broke out, her small cottage was considered unsafe, so she went to live with her sister, Flo, who lived nearby in a large Victorian house.

When the raids were at their height, they both went down to the basement for safety. During one bad air raid, my Grandmother decided she was going to stay in her own bed, but her sister went to the basement as usual. That night their house was bombed, and my Grandmother was saved because the wardrobe fell across her bed, and as the house collapsed, she fell down inside the wardrobe. Her sister in the basement was tragically buried in the rubble and killed.

I was taken to see her in hospital and recall her lying in bed, her lovely grey hair full of ceiling dust. She recovered well, but all her possessions were

Grandmother Alice (right) and sister Flo

lost but one. The only thing she salvaged from the wreckage was a photograph of my brother who was in the Royal Navy. The photo and glass were intact, despite falling from the third floor.

Pamela Webster, Croydon, Surrey

Cookery for you

WARM WINTER SALAD WITH BEETROOT & GOAT'S CHEESE

Serves 2

- ◆ 3 (200 g) fresh beetroots
- ◆ 225 g (8 oz) curly kale (Cavolo Nero), shredded
- ◆ 1 orange
- ◆ 2 tablespoons walnut oil
- ◆ 1 tablespoon balsamic vinegar
- ◆ 1 tablespoon honey
- ◆ 110 g (4 oz) soft goat's cheese

1 In a saucepan, cover the beetroot with water, bring to the boil and simmer for 20-25 minutes, or until tender. Cool, peel and cut into wedges.

2 Meanwhile, boil the kale for 6-8 minutes and drain.

3 Segment the orange, reserving the excess juice. Whisk this juice with the oil, vinegar, honey and seasoning. In a large bowl, toss the kale, beetroot and orange segments in the dressing.

4 Crumble the goat's cheese on top of the salad and serve immediately.

Tips: To save time, use pickled beetroot. For a nutty variation, serve sprinkled with 50 g (2 oz) toasted walnut pieces.

Recipe courtesy www.discoverkale.co.uk

Colourful climbers
Clematis orientalis

Although the yellow candied-peel blooms of Clematis orientalis are a delight in early autumn, it's the fluffy seed heads that follow which really catch the eye. Dancing prettily in the breeze, they look wonderful in the sunlight on a crisp winter's morning. Enjoy the display until March, then prune the plant hard back. Clematis orientalis thrives in sun or partial shade and may reach 6m in height. Plants widely available.

THAT'S INTERESTING...

Here's a good way of remembering the colours of the rainbow, Red, Orange, Yellow, Green, Blue, Indigo and Violet – 'Richard Of York Gave Battle In Vain'

TOP TIP

Brown wrapping paper or old comics make great wrapping for presents. Complete the parcel by tying it up with string and using brown labels.

Healthier for longer!

Get some winter sun – if you can, head to sunnier climes for a good dose of vitamin D, which could help slow down the ageing process and help you prevent a whole host of diseases such as osteoporosis and even some cancers. Your skin makes this essential nutrient from the sun's rays.

West Wales: Dylan Thomas Country

The wild west

Swansea's most famous son is celebrated at the Dylan Thomas Centre where visitors can experience audio-visual displays as well as view the poet's typewriter, letters and scripts. Dylan Thomas was born in the town on October 27 1914 and lived with his family at 5 Cwmdonkin Drive.

As a young man, he went to live in England but returned to Wales with his wife Caitlin to live in the sleepy seaside resort of Laugharne in Pembrokeshire. The couple occupied various residences in the town before settling in The Boathouse which was bought for them by a generous benefactor in 1949. Now open to visitors,

The Boathouse commands spectacular views over the estuary and admirers of his poetry can see the cliff top shed that Thomas used as a writing room. He and Caitlin are both buried in the grounds of nearby St Martin's Church, although he died in New York in 1953.

Dylan Thomas spent many holidays on the coast of Cardigan and was well acquainted with the picturesque seaport of New Quay which has been claimed to be the inspiration for the town of Llareggub in his best loved work, Under Milk Wood. The Black Lion Hotel was a favourite haunt of Thomas' and houses a collection of his memorabilia. Across the road is Gomer House, once the

home of Captain Tom Polly who became Captain Cat in the play.

Other attractions in this part of Wales range from the spectacular Gower coast close to Swansea to heritage sites such as Pembroke Castle. Walkers can stride out across the Black Mountains (part of the Brecon Beacons National Park) while shoppers will enjoy searching for souvenirs in the many arts and crafts outlets across the region.

Remember, remember

Ah! Happy days

Bonfire Night was an exciting time for Mrs Joyce Clifford of Dymock, Gloucestershire

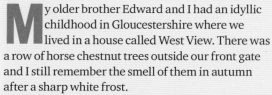

My older brother Edward and I had an idyllic childhood in Gloucestershire where we lived in a house called West View. There was a row of horse chestnut trees outside our front gate and I still remember the smell of them in autumn after a sharp white frost.

I was a tomboy and could climb any tree as fast as any boy. I tried to tag along with Edward and his friends but that didn't go down too well except for the days before November 5 when they would let me help them make the bonfire.

And what a bonfire it was, too! We used to go to the sawmills to get some large tyres and bowl them home. Wood blocks were transported in a truck that my father had made from a large wooden box on two wheels. Father's trees would also get 'pruned' to provide us with branches. (This often went

unnoticed until it was too late.) And we swept up all the horse chestnut tree leaves to add to the pile which, when it was finished, stood at least twenty feet high.

We also made a Guy Fawkes and sat him on top of the fire (we needed a ladder to get up there) with a rocket in his hat. Fireworks weren't so plentiful in those days: Edward and his friends had to catch the bus to Gloucester where they queued for hours at a shop called Fletchers. They were only allowed a limited number each but by putting them all together they made a nice display.

We were all so excited when the great day dawned – half the population of the village turned out to watch. Everyone had a wonderful evening and we could bake potatoes in the hot ashes for two days afterwards.

Sing along

Can you match these movie songs to the films they came from? If you get stuck the answers are below.

1.	Raindrops Are Falling On My Head	A.	An American In Paris
2.	Whatever Will Be, Will Be (Que Sera, Sera)	B.	Annie
3.	True Love	C.	Annie Get Your Gun
4.	I Wanna Be Loved By You	D.	Breakfast At Tiffany's
5.	Tomorrow	E.	Butch Cassidy and the Sundance Kid
6.	As Time Goes By	F.	Calamity Jane
7.	Oh, What a Beautiful Morning	G.	Casablanca
8.	I Want To Be Like You	H.	Easter Parade
9.	Buffalo Gal (Won't You Come Out Tonight)	I.	Funny Girl
10.	Don't Rain On My Parade	J.	High Society
11.	Getting To Know You	K.	Holiday Inn
12.	Good Morning	L.	It's A Wonderful Life
13.	Have Yourself A Merry Little Christmas	M.	Meet Me In St Louis
14.	I Got Rhythm	N.	Oklahoma!
15.	Secret Love	O.	Play Misty For Me
16.	Moon River	P.	Singin' In The Rain
17.	Steppin' Out With My Baby	Q.	Some Like It Hot
18.	The First Time Ever I Saw Tour Face	R.	The Jungle Book
19.	White Christmas	S.	The King And I
20.	Anything You Can Do (I Can Do Better)	T.	The Man Who New Too Much

Answers: 1E, 2T, 3J, 4Q, 5B, 6G, 7N, 8R, 9L, 10I, 11S, 12P, 13M, 14A, 15F, 16D, 17H, 18O, 19K, 20C.

A shampoo and set,

Hairdressing in the 1960s – remember Marcel waves, pin curls and blue roots? Jean Daïf does...

We lived in Kent until I was almost 16, then my parents decided to move to London; it was 1961, the sixties were about to swing and my first job beckoned.

Hairdressing was something I'd always wanted to do, several bald dolls testifying to this. So it was very exciting when I was lucky enough to be offered an apprenticeship at a really smart salon in West London. It was in a great location – Shepherd's Bush television studios were just down the road, so we had an interesting clientele – well known actresses, budding actresses and a lot of well connected ladies.

One of our famous clients was Hattie Jacques, who was a really lovely, down-to-earth lady. Another was a well-known actress/comedienne still on our screens today, who was a great character. If she was kept waiting for her appointment, she would grab a bowl and brush, to mix up, and apply her water tint herself.

The Russian ambassador's wife was another client. She always preferred me to shampoo her, as she thought I did the most thorough job. She very kindly gave me a signed picture of Valentina Tereshkova, the first lady in space. We were delighted!

At first, all I did was sweep hair trimmings, fold towels and make the tea. After a few weeks, I began the shampoo training. I enjoyed shampooing, even though my hands became red raw. I smothered them in barrier cream, and eventually my skin became used to all the different products. I wasn't allowed near a pair of scissors for weeks, and even then I had to learn how to hold them properly first.

Then there were the 'Model nights'. Volunteers would come in and we were taught, and had to practise Marcel waving, pin curling and setting hair in rollers.

Marvel waving was a method of waving hair using the fingers to push the waves into place, then securing them with metal clips – particularly difficult on absolutely straight hair. Pin curling was easier; forming small pieces of hair into little circles, and clipping the root end with a metal clip. We had to make sure the hair was smoothly clipped, otherwise the client's hair would be a ball of frizz.

The wages were very low – I

please

Right: Jean outside the salon, complete with Dr Scholl sandals
Below: Stylist Izzy going home after work

received just two pounds nine shillings and sixpence, but I did receive tips, so I got by somehow. A shampoo and set cost ten shillings and sixpence, cutting from seven shillings and sixpence, and permanent colouring from two guineas.

There were several other apprentices – Dianne, Christine, Sue, Sandra and Adele – my best friend.

We had a lot of laughs, especially when something went wrong. Among the various mishaps was when an expensive pearl necklace was cut through by a stylist who was trimming a very well-to-do lady's hair. The necklace stayed in place, though, because of the towel round the client's neck.

When she took it off, the pearls scattered everywhere. We scrabbled round until all the pearls were found. Fortunately, the lady thought the necklace, which was a family heirloom, had come apart due to its age.

One mistake was down to me. I'd just learned how to mix up and apply hair colour, and the clients had their formulae written out on cards. This particular client

was a well-known model who did television adverts. I misread the card and put Ash Blue in the mixing bowl instead of Ash Blonde (the Blue was mixed with Black hair dye to make it a softer colour).

When the lady's roots turned a vibrant shade of blue, I almost fainted! Luckily, she was totally absorbed in a magazine, and she was rather short-sighted. I quickly wrapped a towel around her

head and went for help. One of the stylists applied a very strong bleach, telling the lady that her roots were taking longer to 'lift' this time. Happily, the colour came out even better than usual. I was always very careful to read the cards properly after that!

I stayed at the salon until 1968 when I married. My next job I kept for years – as a wife and mother.

I wonder if Marcel waving and pin curling are still part of a hairdresser's training today? If not, they don't know what they're missing!

We scrabbled round until all the pearls were found

Tuesday
1

Saturday
12

Wednesday
2

Sunday
13

Thursday
3

Monday
14

Friday
4

Tuesday
15

Saturday
5

Wednesday
16

Sunday
6

Thursday
17

Monday
7

Friday
18

Tuesday
8

Saturday
19

Wednesday
9

Sunday
20

Thursday
10

Monday
21

Friday
11

Tuesday
22

Wednesday	Monday
23	**28**
	Bank Holiday (in lieu of Dec 26)
Thursday	Tuesday
24	**29**
Christmas Eve	
Friday	Wednesday
25	**30**
Christmas day	
Saturday	Thursday
26	**31**
Boxing Day	New Year's Eve
Sunday	
27	

Behind the Scenes

Let's Make Love, 1960

Marilyn Monroe on the set of Let's Make Love in 1960 gives a luminous flirtatious look (even when she wasn't in front of the movie camera) at Gene Kelly, with Yves Montand on her right, lost in thought, and a cigarette…

Completed two years before her death in 1962, the plot of

Let's Make Love revolves around billionaire Jean-Marc Clement (Montand) who finds himself in a show with Amanda Dell (Marilyn). He tries desperately to improve his stage presence, hiring teachers – Bing Crosby for singing, Gene Kelly for dancing and Milton

Berle for comedy – in order to win Amanda's heart.

Directed by the great George Cukor, Frankie Vaughan also appears in the film, singing several numbers with Marilyn, who also sings that great Cole Porter song, My Heart Belongs To Daddy.

Cookery for you

RICH CHOCOLATE SHORTBREAD

Makes 12

- ◆ 225 g (8 oz) unsalted butter
- ◆ 6 tablespoons Splenda® granulated sweetener
- ◆ 60 g (2½ oz) caster sugar
- ◆ ½ teaspoon vanilla extract
- ◆ 6 tablespoons cocoa powder
- ◆ 250 g (9 oz) plain flour

1 Preheat the oven to 170°C/325°F/Gas mark 3. Line two baking trays with non-stick parchment.

2 Place the butter, granulated sweetener, sugar and vanilla extract in a large bowl. Using an electric whisk, beat until smooth and lighter in colour.

3 Gradually sift in the cocoa and flour, and beat again until well combined.

4 Divide the dough in two, and using your hands, press out two 15 cm (6 in) diameter rounds. Prick all over and mark a pattern around the edges with a fork.

5 Bake for 15-20 minutes, or until it's beginning to brown. Remove from the oven and immediately cut each round into 6 slices.

6 Leave to cool on the tray before transferring to an airtight container.

Recipe courtesy Splenda®, www.splenda.co.uk

■ THAT'S INTERESTING...

Dalmatian puppies are born without spots.

My Grandparents

My Grandparents, Annie and Frederick Batt, lived in a terraced house in Hamworthy, Poole, Dorset, and from their upstairs back window you could see Poole Harbour.

'Granfy' was Poole Town Football Club's trainer and physiotherapist for Poole Pirates Speedway. He had a large garden and two allotments, growing vegetables – including the biggest onions you could imagine – and flowers, including wonderful sweet peas; I was so proud taking a bunch to school. At the bottom of their garden they kept chickens, and hatched the chicks in incubators in the garden shed.

He would sit me on his knee, sat in his big wooden chair and sing Danny Boy while Granny was busy in the kitchen baking; pies, cakes, bottling fruit and vegetables, salting runner beans and making homemade wine – elderberry, damson, gooseberry and parsnip.

Once a week my friend Doreen and I would visit them for the day, and every time, travelling over on the No 89 bus, we would say, 'I bet we have apple pie today,' and we always did – a huge and delicious apple pie! Nobody could make one as good as Granny!

Jackie Wright, Poole, Dorset

Top: Jackie and Granfy sitting in his big wooden armchair
Above: Jackie and her family at Christmas

■ TOP TIP

To keep your hands well moisturised, put on hand cream before putting on your rubber gloves.

Ms Denison, Rhyl, North Wales

Colourful climbers
Happy wanderer

Hardenbergia is a tender evergreen, twining climber that thrives in a sunny conservatory, as long as the compost doesn't dry out. Producing woody stems and bunches of purple pea-like flowers followed by attractive seed pods, it blooms happily in mid winter when under glass. Plant it at the base of decorative trellis and it will put on 3m of growth. Seeds are available from Jungle Seeds at www.jungleseeds.co.uk

Healthier for longer!

Make love more! – Couples who have sex three times a week look on average 10 years younger than couples who make love twice a week say Scottish scientists. It's the feel good chemicals that sex releases that provide the benefits.

Meeting the stars

In 1956, when I was 12, a children's newspaper was running a series granting children's wishes.

I'd always loved Mr Pastry, and after seeing the funny sketch where he danced The Lancers by himself, I dreamed I'd danced it with him, and so wrote to the paper about it.

To my delight, they contacted my parents and I was taken to Elstree Studios where the man himself (Richard Hearne) was making a film. We were able to dance a few steps together before he had to go back to filming.

What a lovely man he was, chatting to me like an old friend instead of an awkward schoolgirl. I have never forgotten that wonderful day and what a down-to-earth, lovable person Richard Hearne was.

Marion Twyman, Rochester, Kent

Marion and Mr Pastry stepping out

Schooldays remembered

The primary school I went to – St Matthews – had a headmaster called Mr Scholar, which we all thought was most appropriate.

The photograph is of our Christmas play in 1952. On the evening of the play there was a real 'pea souper' fog outside so our parents had to bring us to school to make sure we didn't get lost!

The play was called The Three Scarecrows and we were all very excited when the following week

The Three Scarecrows

a photo appeared in the local paper. I'm the child right in the middle.

My sister still attends the school on a daily basis, the only difference being now she's the playground supervisor!

Valerie Swadling, Bognor Regis, W Sussex

Cookery for you

Colourful climbers
Jasminum nudiflorum

Winter jasmine is a popular shrub and is widely grown against walls. Unlike many other varieties of jasmine, it doesn't twine, so will need tying-in if grown vertically. The bright green stems make it appear evergreen, even in winter when the tiny bright yellow blooms arrive. It thrives in sun or partial shade and blooms between December and March. Regular pruning keeps it under control and prevents bare patches from developing. It may reach 3m in height. Plants widely available.

BROCCOLI TOSSED IN BUTTER WITH CHESTNUTS AND PANCETTA
Serves 4

◆ 400 g (13 oz) Tenderstem® broccoli, cut into 6cm (2½ inch) strips
◆ 50 g (2 oz) unsalted butter
◆ 75 g (3 oz) pancetta lardons
◆ 200 g (7 oz) cooked chestnuts, roughly chopped
◆ Salt and cracked black pepper

1 Bring a medium-sized pan of water to the boil, add the broccoli and cook for 30 seconds. Drain, then cool under cold running water. Set aside.
2 Heat a medium-sized frying pan and add the butter and lardons. Cook until the lardons start to release some fat and turn golden brown, or about 5 minutes.
3 Add the chestnuts and broccoli to the pan. Cook for a further 2 minutes, season with salt, plenty of pepper and serve immediately.

Tips: Makes a great accompanying dish to roasts, or as a festive lunch with some crusty bread.

Healthier for longer!

Go crazy for cranberries – they do more than just prevent cystitis according to scientists in Tel Aviv. Cranberries contain a substance that stops bacteria sticking to the surfaces in your body – so they're thought to help prevent tooth cavities, the flu and reduce the risk of gastric ulcers. The bad news is – it only seems to work for women!

Recipe courtesy Tenderstem® broccoli, www.tenderstem.co.uk

My Grandparents

I was born in Newport, Monmouthshire and was fortunate to know both sets of Grandparents.

Nana Kate lived on the other side of town, so we'd take a penny tram ride to visit her. She was a real lady, a regular chapelgoer and greatly respected. She did, however, marry 'beneath herself' to a veteran of the Boer War. Granddad looked like Oliver Hardy, and spoke with a booming voice which frightened us – he'd been a Sergeant Major in the Welsh Regiment.

Although poor Nana kept herself spotless, it was hard as she had just a cold pump in the yard. She would boil her hankies in a saucepan on the fire, and each week would buy rosewater and glycerine which the chemist would put into her own bottle, and which was sprinkled over her undies.

Each week, she'd visit my mother, and when we came home from school, the scent of Nan's rosewater would drift down the passage from the front door, so we knew at once she was there.

**Olive Bradbury,
Llandudno, Gwynedd**

Grandma Kate

Schooldays remembered

Netball team captain, 16-year-old Carole, holding the ball

I started school in 1949 with a big grin on my face, and it never faded until the day I left when I cried my eyes out.

I always enjoyed English, sport and drama right from the beginning. My first part in a school production was as a witch, complete with broomstick. I also took part in the Christmas nativity plays, and was a shepherd one year. I remember giving the baby Jesus a loaf of bread. It was a small brown pottery loaf – I don't know how he would have eaten it, or if brown loaves were around then but it raised a laugh.

Netball was my favourite sport, and I was lucky to be selected for the junior school team. As captain, I was delighted to collect the shield for winning the divisional rally, on behalf of the school.

My netball career extended to senior school, once again as captain. I could have played netball all day, every day, and I remember my PE teacher saying, when we had to do gymnastics, 'You can't play netball all the time, Carole'.

I was Head Girl in my final year at senior school and was over the moon to be chosen. There was one drawback, however, I had to answer the phone in the headmaster's office when he was out of the school. We didn't have a telephone at home, and I wasn't used to answering one. I used to sit there, praying it wouldn't ring, but it usually did.

Carole Sparrow, Hockley, Essex

Cookery for you

BOXING DAY TRIFLE

Serves 4

- ◆ 2 tablespoons brandy
- ◆ 2 tablespoons raisins
- ◆ 450 g (1 lb) cooked Christmas pudding, leftovers are great for this
- ◆ 4 tablespoons cranberry sauce
- ◆ 425 g (13 oz) ready-made custard
- ◆ Anchor extra thick cream with Courvoisier VS Cognac

1 Put the brandy and raisins into a small bowl and soak for at least 1 hour – then sprinkle onto the bottom of a large deep dish.

2 Slice the Christmas pudding into medium thick slices and place in the dish.

3 Drizzle over the cranberry sauce to roughly cover the pudding slices.

4 Spoon over the custard and finish off with a thick layer of Anchor Extra Thick Cream with Courvoisier VS Cognac.

5 Chill in the fridge, then serve.

Recipe courtesy Anchor cream www.anchorsquirtymoments.co.uk

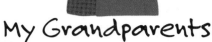

My Grandparents

Daisy and Walter Lewis, maternal grandparents

Margaret's paternal grandparents, Alice and Bill Hawkins

I was lucky to grow up with all four of my grandparents, and have many wonderful memories of them all.

My earliest memory of my paternal grandparents was in 1946 when I was three years old. I'd had whooping cough and they took me on holiday to convalesce, to Nefyn in Wales.

We stayed in a rented bungalow on the cliffs overlooking the sea, and I remember walking along the beach holding Granddad's hand and looking up to see my Nan calling us in for tea. This was my first holiday, and my first sight of the sea, which I have loved ever since.

One Christmas morning, my sister Pat and I woke to find a beautiful dolls' cot by our beds. My Granddad Lewis had made it from orange boxes, painted it pink and put transfers on the side. My Nan Lewis had made a mattress, sheets and blankets and a pillow each end.

Granddad Hawkins had bought us a doll each, and Nan Hawkins had made all the dolls' clothes. What a wonderful present!

Margaret Berry, Ferndown, Dorset

THAT'S INTERESTING...

Carols came from France in about 1300 and were once sung at all feast days during the year.

Schooldays remembered

My family lived at Harebeating Farm, near Hailsham, Sussex, and my schooldays began in 1937, when I attended the infants' school in the High Street. For the first week or so, my mother took me the mile to school using the footpath across four fields if it was fine. If not, it was a long detour.

Six-year-old Bernard

In July 1939 my brother Alan was born at the farm. I thought it was strange that morning that my father woke me up to go to school, and as we had to pass through my parents' bedroom to get downstairs, he said: "Don't make a noise, you have a new baby brother."

That summer I moved on to junior school, a mile further to walk but a more up-to-date school, and from our classroom we had a panoramic view of the South Downs. Our headmistress was a formidable middle-aged lady called Miss Rous, who'd also been my father's teacher.

By now the war had begun, and one morning my seven-year-old brother Raymond and I were walking to school when a lady shouted from her upstairs window to take cover behind her garden wall. Just as we lay down, two German fighter planes roared over at rooftop height, firing their guns as they went. It was all over in a few moments, and we then continued on our way to school.

Bernard E French, Burgess Hill, West Sussex

Healthier for longer!

Make time for friends – having a wide social group could help you to live longer, according to Australian scientists. People with lots of friends are more likely to live healthier, happier lives – and so will live longer.

Meeting the stars

I used to work in a sheltered housing scheme in Woburn Sands, and one year Ted Rogers came to switch on the Christmas lights in the High Street. The next year Bob Monkhouse came to do the honours; he came to meet the residents and, just like Ted, he was a really lovely man.

Brenda Hall, Milton Keynes, Bucks

Brenda and Bob Monkhouse

Colourful climbers
Cotoneaster

Although Cotoneaster horizontalis makes a great garden shrub, the characteristic herringbone pattern of its stems ensures it looks even better when trained against a wall. With cream flowers in late spring and autumn berries that last all winter – hungry birds allowing – it is worth growing in every garden. It thrives in sun or partial shade and should reach 50cm in height when planted against a wall. Plants widely available.

Schooldays remembered

Gwen, aged five in 1952, and she's not sure about the hair-do...

Christmas was coming! We'd spent weeks perfecting our crêpe paper hats with help from our teacher, Miss Groom, who embellished them all with silver and gold paint. My mother was also determined I should have a memorable day and produced a cornflower blue taffeta dress for me to wear, and (against my wishes) she curled my naturally straight hair with tongs heated up in the fire.

The party was held at the village hall just a short walk from school, and when we walked in, it was an awesome sight – the Christmas tree and paper chain decorations, the large table full of sandwiches – egg and meat paste – fancy cakes and crackers.

After we'd made light work of the food we played games and sang our well practised carols for parents who had arrived to take us home. But the day was not yet over, as we were waiting for Santa at 6 o'clock.

Every child had a present of games or drawing books and we were all thrilled with whatever we received. Two of my older sisters came to collect me and we walked home two miles along a dark road but I was still thinking about what a wonderful day it had been.

**Gwendolyn Cooper,
Swadlincote, Derbys**

My Grandparents

My grandparents lived in Mistley, Essex and had four daughters and three sons – my mother was the eldest daughter.

My parents, two sisters and I always spent Christmas at my grandparents' house, together with my mother's sisters and brothers, and my cousins. One of my uncles had a house next door, which was a great help when it came to sleeping arrangements – often we slept five to a bed!

There was often more than 21 of us for Christmas dinner, all squashed round a large table, with four children on a small side table. My Grandma had a maid, which was a great help.

Marion's Grandma Agness and Granddad William (front) with their seven children, taken in 1950

After dinner, Grandma would have all the grandchildren round the table, then she'd get out six small wooden moneyboxes. She'd collected farthings over the year for us, and we'd all receive about three shillings each.

When we made too much noise, my dear Granddad would bang his walking stick on the floor and say, 'Hark! Hark!'

Our youngest uncles weren't much older than us, and would play tricks on each other, and put stink bombs in my grandparents' bedrooms.

I still love Christmas and to have the family together.

**Marion Ward,
Colchester, Essex**

Cookery for you

THE 'ULTIMATE' ROAST POTATOES

Serves 4

- ◆ 8 medium roasting potatoes, peeled and cut in halves.
- ◆ 1 tablespoon goose fat for every 50 g (2 oz) potato
- ◆ Salt and pepper

1 Pre-heat the oven to 200°C/400°F/Gas Mark 6.
2 Parboil the potatoes for 8-10 minutes, drain and put them back in the pan with the cover. Shake pan to rough up the edges and season.
3 Put the goose fat into a roasting tray and heat in the hot oven until the fat is smoking.
4 Remove from the oven and carefully place the potatoes into the tray and coat them with the fat. Roast for 45 minutes, or until crisp and golden. Baste and turn the potatoes at frequent intervals.

Tip: Other vegetables also taste great roasted in goose fat, try roasting parsnips to add a delicious twist to this classic Christmas accompaniment.

Recipe courtesy The Goose Fat Information Service

Colourful climbers
Streptosolon

Enthusiastic gardeners love trying unusual plants, so why not give the tender climber Streptosolon jasminoides a go? It's extremely rare in this country because it requires a heated conservatory, but repays any TLC with terminal clusters of warmly orange flowers in mid winter and sporadically throughout the year. Seeds are available from Jungle Seeds at www.jungleseeds.co.uk

THAT'S INTERESTING...

Boxing Day takes its name from the clay alms boxes put outside churches during the Christmas period, which were broken open on the 26th and their contents distributed to the poor.

TOP TIP

Now's the time to be thinking of the January sales – to buy next year's Christmas cards, and to make a start on the presents!

Healthier for longer!

Have a laugh – people with a sense of humour outlive those who don't find life amusing, say researchers in Norway. It's thought that humour helps you deal with stress and anxiety and keeps your immune system healthy.

Kent: Charles Dickens Country

Victorian vistas

Born in Portsmouth in 1812, Charles Dickens moved to Chatham with his family when he was five and it was here that he spent the happiest years of his childhood. The family eventually moved away but Dickens never forgot his love of Kent, returning frequently to Broadstairs for holidays with his wife and children.

The Dickens House Museum in Broadstairs was once the home of a Miss Mary Pearson Strong, said to be the original inspiration for the character of Miss Betsey Trotwood in David Copperfield. Across the bay from here can be seen the forbiddingly castellated building known as Fort House which Dickens had in mind when he wrote Bleak House.

In 1856, when he had become a household name, the great Victorian novelist returned to Kent to reside at Gad's Hill Place, a house near Chatham that he had first admired as a small boy walking past with his father. He died at Gad's Hill in 1870.

Dickens' name is forever associated with Christmas jollity and at the beginning of December the town of Rochester, which has retained much of its Victorian charm, holds an annual festival to celebrate the season.

But for the full Dickens experience, visitors must make their way to Chatham Maritime to discover the Dickens World theme park where Peggotty's old boat house has been recreated and the ghost of Ebenezer Scrooge lurks in the Haunted House.

Kent's other attractions include the lonely Romney Marshes where Magwitch loomed alarmingly out of the mist to frighten Pip in Great Expectations.

Ah! Happy days

Devon was heaven

Peter Relf of Gravesend was a townie who took to country life

In September 1940 my sister Joyce and I were evacuated to the country. Our new home was Western Cottage in the little village of Bucks Cross on the coast of north Devon. Although Joyce returned to London after six months, I stayed for two years and look back on them as some of the happiest of my life.

I attended the local school where the milk was brought to the top of the road in a churn and two of the older lads had to fetch it from the crossroad. It was then ladled into cups which, in winter, would be stood all around the big stove in the classroom so that it was warm by playtime.

In my leisure time I had what seemed to me the world's largest playground to amuse myself in. I used to wander through the woods alone, armed with my bow and arrows. I acquired a mole trap and used to make traps for rabbits from string and pieces of wood. The moles and rabbits had no need to fear me as I never caught anything.

The nearest the war came to us was when a German plane dropped two mines in a field just outside Bideford.

Christmas meant a party at the village hall for all the children, including the evacuees. A tree that almost reached the ceiling was put in the centre of the hall, decorated with real candles. On the tree would be a present for every child from Squire Elweys who lived at the big house.